THE RAF BATTLE *of* BRITAIN FIGHTER PILOT'S KITBAG

UNIFORMS & EQUIPMENT FROM THE SUMMER OF 1940 AND THE HUMAN STORIES BEHIND THEM

Also by Mark Hillier

Westhampnett at War

To War in a Spitfire

Joe Roddis: In Support of the Few

Suitcases, Vultures and Spies: From Bomber Command to Special Operations
*The Story of Wing Commander Thomas Murray DSO DFC**

A Fighter Command Station at War: A Photographic Record of RAF Westhampnett
from the Battle of Britain to D-Day and Beyond

War Birds: the Diary of a Great War Pilot

THE RAF BATTLE *of* BRITAIN FIGHTER PILOT'S KITBAG

UNIFORMS & EQUIPMENT FROM THE SUMMER OF 1940 AND THE HUMAN STORIES BEHIND THEM

Mark Hillier

FRONTLINE
BOOKS

THE RAF BATTLE OF BRITAIN FIGHTER PILOT'S KITBAG
Uniforms & Equipment from the Summer of 1940 and the Human Stories Behind Them

This edition published in 2018
by Frontline Books
An imprint of Pen & Sword Books Limited,
47 Church Street, Barnsley,
South Yorkshire, S70 2AS.

ISBN 978-1-47384-999-0

A CIP catalogue record for this book is
available from the British Library

Typeset in 9.5/12pt Avenir
by Aura Technology and Software Services, India

Printed and bound in India
by Replika Press Pvt. Ltd.

Pen & Sword Books Limited incorporates the imprints of Atlas,
Archaeology, Aviation, Discovery, Family History, Fiction, History, Maritime, Military, Military Classics,
Politics, Select, Transport, True Crime, Air World, Frontline Publishing, Leo Cooper, Remember When,
Seaforth Publishing,
The Praetorian Press, Wharncliffe Local History, Wharncliffe Transport,
Wharncliffe True Crime and White Owl.

For a complete list of Frontline titles please contact
FRONTLINE BOOKS
47 Church Street, Barnsley, South Yorkshire, S70 2AS, United Kingdom
E-mail: info@frontline-books.com
Website: www.frontline-books.com

CONTENTS

This book is dedicated to the memory of the late Joseph 'Joe' Roddis (1921-2017), one of the RAF groundcrew who so valiantly supported the Few.

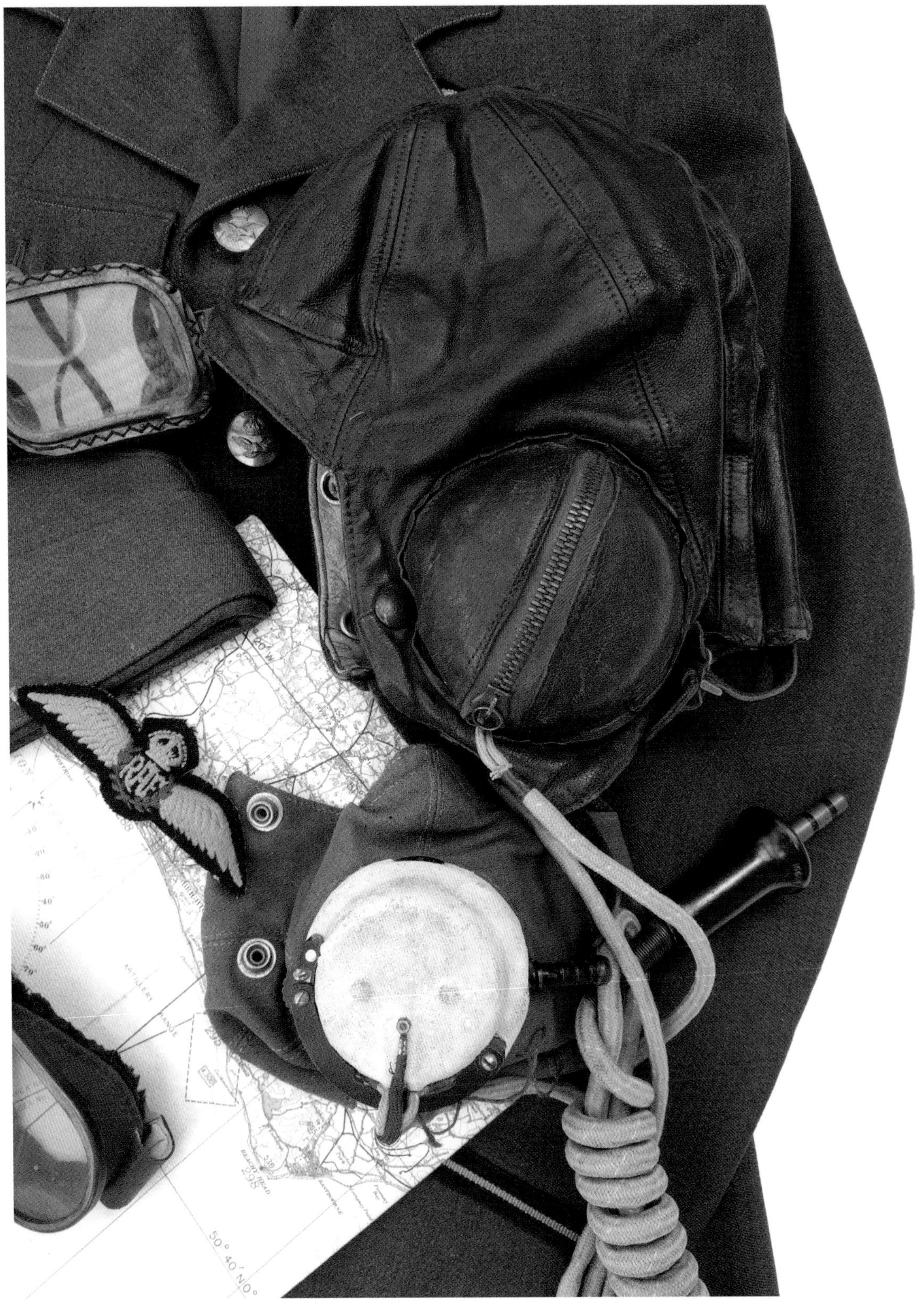

A selection of RAF fighter pilot's clothing and equipment from the Battle of Britain period. (Simon Lannoy Collection)

INTRODUCTION

I have always had a keen interest in the history of the Royal Air Force and, in particular, the Battle of Britain period. I love to read first-hand accounts and have been privileged to meet some of 'The Few' and listen to their stories. I have also been fortunate to have had the opportunity to fly a number of vintage aircraft types representative of those used during flying training by the RAF in the Second World War.

Such experiences have only served to heighten my interest in those dramatic days of 1940, and this has included investigating every aspect of the fighter pilot's clothing and the equipment he was issued with, or was at his disposal. This has led to the discovery of a surprisingly wide assortment of items and artefacts, including personal adaptations of standard kit.

I have chosen to limit the items to those which were used and issued or purchased by those aircrew who were entitled to wear the Battle of Britain Bar to the 1939-45 Star, and covers only the period from 10 July 1940 to 31 October 1940. This would have included pilots flying such iconic aircraft as the Hawker Hurricane and the Supermarine Spitfire, as well as the Boulton Paul Defiant and Bristol Blenheim. The book also includes uniforms from some of the other aircrew from air forces that took part under the command of the RAF such as the Fleet Air Arm, Royal Australian Air Force, Polish, Czech and Free French amongst others.

The Battle of Britain kit bag starts with the headgear, working down to flying clothing and equipment and then lastly uniforms and insignia. Where possible, and where known, the Air Ministry references have been given but it is accepted that many items were private purchase or not official kit. It must also be accepted that this is not a definitive collection and that there may well be other items used during the Battle of Britain which are not featured here.

Mark Hillier,
Fontwell, West Sussex, 2017.

ABOVE LEFT: A typical pilot's equipment during the Battle of Britain, starting at the head with the 'B' Type flying helmet, Mk.IIIA Goggles and D Type oxygen mask. The Irvin jacket and Mae West are worn over the service uniform. The boots are 1939 Pattern. (Simon Lannoy Collection)

ABOVE RIGHT: The typical attire for a Blenheim or Defiant crew member, the Irvin Harness suit worn over the service uniform to save space, again a B Type flying helmet, but this time Mk.III goggles with the broader padding round the lenses. Note also the earlier 1936 pattern flying boot. (Simon Lannoy Collection)

ACKNOWLEDGEMENTS

Without the established research and work carried out by Mick J. Prodger, and his ongoing support, this publication would not have been possible. Also, the expertise and guidance of experienced collectors such as Simon Lannoy and Phil Phillips, who have given their valued time and knowledge, has been invaluable. Thanks must also go to my long-suffering wife Kate and my two lovely children, Molly and George, for their continued support.

Section 1
FLYING HELMETS

Leather flying helmets became available during the very early stages in the history of aviation, offering a degree of protection from the elements and keeping the head warm from the icy blasts encountered in open cockpit aircraft.

As aircraft and the equipment they carried developed, helmet design also progressed. In due course, some had modifications to take a 'Gosport' tube, a chrome or stainless-steel earpiece that connected to a speaking tube to allow conversation with other individuals in an aircraft. Wind and engine noise was, however, frequently a limiting factor for the effectiveness of this method.

By the time the RAF had moved on to higher performance monoplanes that could operate at high altitude, the helmet had to include the ability to connect to an oxygen mask or microphone for communication and take earpieces so that the pilot could communicate using radio transmissions.

The mainstay for the Battle of Britain was the B Type flying helmet. Group Captain Bobby Oxspring DFC, AFC once recalled how his morning duties included setting up his cockpit and checking his helmet to ensure all was ready in case he was scrambled: 'The next move was to carefully arrange the safety harness and parachute straps, plug in the helmet leads to radio and oxygen so that on a scramble the least possible time would be lost in getting strapped in and away. Quick checks to see that the oxygen was flowing through the mask.'[1]

B TYPE FLYING HELMET
Stores Reference: 22c/65, Later re-designated 22C/285-288 in 1941
(The suffix 'C' stands for 'Consumable')

Perhaps the most iconic item of flying clothing issued to Battle of Britain aircrew, the B Type flying helmet understandably features in numerous period photographs.

This helmet was crafted by various tailors, hatters and shoemakers and the labels found within are marked with such names as H. Bednall, Frank Bryan, J. Compton Sons and Webb, Patterson and Stone, Reliance, Robinson and Ensum, B. Sterling, Waddington, and Wareings. The earliest dates found on the labels inside the helmet stitched to the chamois leather interior date back to 1935.

The helmet itself was provided with two separate earphone cups with brass zips which would be stitched into place for the individual fitting. These had their own stores references (22c/66), as did the inserts or sponge rubber cushions (stores ref 22c/67) that helped to reduce noise interference in each cup.

The B Type helmet is split at the back and adjusted by a leather strap. The chin strap is again adjustable and fastened by a friction type 'Bennett' Buckle (the buckle being leather covered). The front of the helmet was provided with two female snap fasteners for use with the D Type oxygen mask typical of the Battle of Britain Period (stores ref: 6D/105). This helmet design was produced in four different sizes.

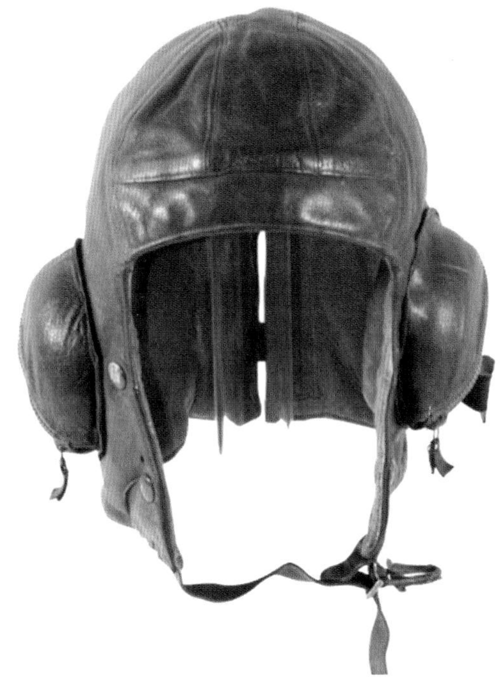

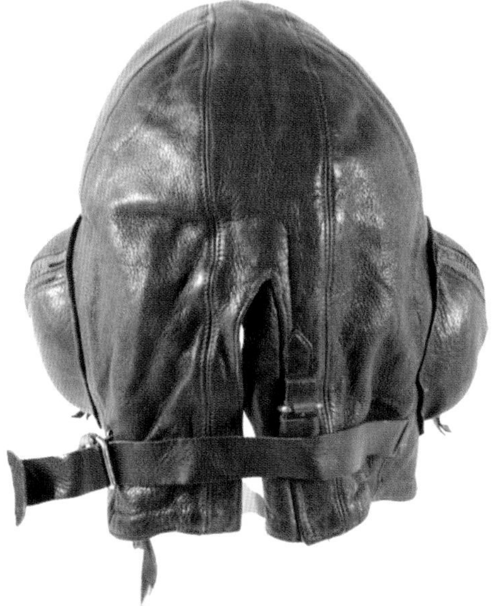

ABOVE: The iconic B Type helmet with separate sew on ear cups, leather chin strap and two female fasteners for the oxygen mask. Note the leather strap and Bennett buckle lower right. (Simon Lannoy Collection)

LEFT: A rear view of the B Type flying helmet showing the split at the back and the adjustment strap. (Simon Lannoy Collection)

Section 2
FLYING GOGGLES

Like helmets, flying goggles were an essential piece of kit for the early aviator. However, as cockpits became enclosed, goggles did not really serve the same purpose for all stages of flight, though pilots might still take off and land with the canopy open for safety reasons. If, during combat, the pilot of a Hurricane or Spitfire suffered damage to the engine they could end up with hot oil over the windshield, perhaps necessitating a landing with the hood open, for which goggles would again be important.

During combat goggles would offer some protection to an airman's eyes from dust and grit floating around the cockpit during high energy manoeuvres such as in combat with a Bf 109. Equally, if the aircraft was damaged or hit, goggles gave a degree of protection against shrapnel, shell or bullet fragments, bits of Perspex from the canopy, or glass from the instruments. In the worst possible scenarios, where fire occurred in the cockpit, they could help prevent serious damage to the eyes.

One pilot who was seriously burned during the Battle of Britain was Flight Lieutenant Richard Hope Hillary of 603 (City of Edinburgh) Squadron. On 3 September 1940, Hillary had been vectored to intercept an incoming raid, though his squadron was outnumbered and the enemy had a height advantage. Hillary took evasive action and tried to climb for height when he noticed another Bf 109:

'Then, just below me and to my left, I saw what I had been praying for – a Messerschmitt climbing and away from the sun. I closed in to 200 yards, and from slightly to one side gave him a two-second burst: fabric ripped off the wing and black smoke poured from the engine, but he did not go down. Like a fool, I did not break away, but put in another three-second burst. Red flames shot upwards and he spiralled out of sight.

'At that moment, I felt a terrific explosion which knocked the control stick from my hand, and the whole machine quivered like a stricken animal. In a second, the cockpit was a mass of flames: instinctively, I reached up to open the hood. It would not move. I tore off my straps and managed to force it back; but this took time, and when I dropped back into the seat and reached for the stick in an effort to turn the plane on its back, the heat was so intense that I could feel myself going. I remember a second of sharp agony, remember thinking "So this is it!" and putting both hands to my eyes. Then I passed out.'[2]

One of the other pilots who was flying with Hillary that day was Squadron Leader Basil Gerald Stapleton DFC, DFC. Stapleton was certain why Hillary's burns were worse than they might have been:

'He didn't wear his goggles so the burns occurred from the forehead down to his nose. It is possible that his top lip may have been burnt when he took his oxygen mask off, which would have been as stupid as not wearing goggles, but what is more likely is that the flames that seared his lip were drawn in and fed on the flow of the flammable oxygen that continued to flow to his mask during his attempts to free himself from the inferno of the cockpit.'[3]

Despite Stapleton's comments, the Mk.III and Mk.IIIa goggles where not entirely ideal for protection against fire and heat as they were made of celluloid. Consequently, some pilots decided to not wear goggles as they were not keen on the examples available. In due course, the Air Ministry returned to flat, laminated glass goggles, in the form of the Mk.IV, which gave better protection.

If the pilots and aircrew wore their gloves and goggles it would at least offer some protection for a limited time, but intense heat could be extreme, as experienced by Group Captain Thomas Percy Gleave CBE. Gleave was shot down whilst flying a Hurricane, and recalled how 'the flames increased until the cockpit was like the centre of a blow lamp nozzle. There was nothing to do but bale out.'[4]

Air Commodore Peter Brothers CBE, DSO, DFC, also remembers that the cold was a problem: 'At height, cold was a constant problem; the canopy would mist up, and ice used to form inside and out on the front, bullet-proofed windshield. I often had to scrape ice of the glass at the front but I could see out of each side which was made of Perspex. Goggles also used to mist up and were a nuisance, uncomfortable. But they were useful if you had to bale out, and helped prevent burning of the eyes if you were hit'.[5]

GOGGLES, FLYING, LIGHTWEIGHT, POPULARLY KNOWN AS THE Mk.II
Stores Reference: 22c/44

In many photographs of the Battle of Britain period, pilots and crews can be seen wearing a variety of flying goggles, some private purchase, some issue and some that pre-date the period by some years and in effect obsolete.

The lightweight goggles were actually introduced into service in 1928, remaining in use, officially at least, until 1935. It is stated that some pilots before and during the Battle of Britain did not like the Mk.III and Mk IIIa goggles issued to them, and that they therefore sought out old stocks of the Mk.II goggles. The Mk.II goggles have flat, laminated lenses that gave better protection than the Mk.III. Resistant to scratches, the Mk.II lenses sometimes had a blue-green tint.

The Mk.II goggles are edged with simulated fur around the eye pieces. The strap is of a sprung leather construction with two adjustment buckles.

OPPOSITE: Flight Lieutenant Walter 'Farmer' Lawson, one of 19 Squadron's flight commanders, photographed in his flying kit at RAF Fowlmere during late September 1940. As well as his Mae West, he wears a B Type flying helmet, D Type oxygen mask with Mk.19 microphone assembly, and Mk.II Goggles, which were popular as they had clear triplex glass. (Andy Saunders Collection)

ABOVE and BELOW: Despite the fact that the Mk.II goggles were no longer issued after 1935, it seems that as many pilots did not like the replacement Mk.III they sought old stocks of the Mk.IIs and wore them, the latter being optically they less prone to damage and visual distortion. (Phil Phillips Collection)

GOGGLES, FLYING, Mk.III
Stores Reference: 22C/69

Although not very popular, both the Mk.III and Mk.IIIa goggles were the main issue available at the start of the Battle of Britain. The earlier Mk.III goggles, which were introduced around 1935, comprised curved celluloid lenses which were not scratch resistant and also offered very little protection to the wearer should a fire occur in the cockpit.

These goggles had a padded band of leather around the outside of the eyepiece and were originally designed for open cockpit use, with the padded band filling the gap between the pilots face and the helmet. Although they have a sprung strap to retain them in position, they were not practical with the B Type helmet due to the domed ear cups and they would not stay in place.

The frames at the front have two small air intakes at the top near the central hinge to help prevent the build-up of moisture and condensation inside the goggles which could then freeze. The goggles were adjustable by a friction buckle at the rear. The leather strap was stamped with an Air Ministry mark as well as the stores reference and description.

ABOVE and LEFT: A pair of Mk.III goggles photographed on an early B Type flying helmet; the latter is not fitted with earcups. The goggles had celluloid lenses which were susceptible to scratches and offered no protection in a fire. Note the wider padded surround on the googles, these having been designed originally for open cockpit flying, and this offered better fitting to the face. (Phil Phillips Collection)

GOGGLES, FLYING, Mk.IIIA
Stores Reference: 22C/62

This design had a similar appearance to the Mk.III, though they do not have the padded leather surround.

Introduced in 1936, the Mk.IIIa goggles are the most common type seen worn by Battle of Britain aircrew. A subtle design difference is the brass frame being cushioned with padded velvet internally. They also had larger air vents on the front at the hinge. These were designed more for aircraft with enclosed cockpits.

Unfortunately, as with the Mk.III, regular use revealed that these goggles were not ideal, the curved celluloid being easily scratched and could also distort pilots' vision. This is not ideal when judging distances and heights at critical stages of flight, such as landing, when a pilot relies on his peripheral vision. Again, as with the Mk.III, they were not very easy to wear with the B Type helmet due to the position of the ear cups, the goggles would ride up and were not an ideal fit over the eyes.

A pair of Mk.IIIa goggles. These have a similar design to the Mk.III but with less padding around the eyes. The strap is identical. These googles were not a widely popular choice due to the problems with the lenses not being of laminated glass; also they did not tend to work well with the B Type helmet due to the earpiece sticking out and the goggles riding up over the face. (Phil Phillips Collection)

Flight Lieutenant Ian Gleed of 87 Squadron seen here with his Hawker Hurricane which had been decorated with a painting of Figaro, the cat from the Pinocchio story. Gleed is wearing his service uniform, with the rank on his sleeve, a 1932 Pattern life-preserver, B Type flying helmet with D Type oxygen mask and Mk.IIIa flying goggles.

GOGGLES, FLYING, Mk.IV
Stores Reference: 22C/111

These goggles were introduced in June 1940 after the Air Ministry called for a new design which gave improved optical clarity, better protection to the wearer and also an improved fit for use with the B Type flying helmet.

With an angular look and split lenses of laminated glass fitted in hinged lens holders, the Mk.IV goggles are visually distinctive. The body, made of brass and quite heavy, was painted black. The inside was fitted with four sponge rubber pads for a comfortable fit. The goggles also featured a flip down polarized lens, or 'flip-shield', to help look for enemy aircraft in the sun, but these were quite fragile and often broke off.

The lens was secured to the goggles by a spring type hinge. To help with better fitting to the B Type, the Mk.IV featured elasticised ear loops which fitted around the ear pieces on the flying helmet and then a leather tightening strap across the loops at the back. The markings for the goggles are on the rear leather strap.

These goggles were always issued with a set of spare lenses and an accessory wallet. For the MkIVa, a set of helmet guide plates was provided with the accessory kit. Riveted to the sides of the B Type helmet, these helped stop the goggles drop down during high 'G' manoeuvres.

Interestingly, all the models of the Mk.IV goggles are listed as available in Air Ministry Order 614, dated 27 June 1940, and so all are thought to have been available during the Battle of Britain period.[6]

ABOVE and RIGHT: The Mk.IV goggles were introduced in June 1940. The frames were made of brass, and they had triplex glass lenses. The elastic loops were designed to work better with the B Type helmet. They had a flip-down tinted lens but these were fragile and often broke off. Note the hinged lenses which could be changed over, hence the accessory pack. (Simon Lannoy Collection)

GOGGLES, FLYING, Mk.IVA
Stores Reference: 22C/126

This design was made of moulded black bakelite which was very fragile. Moulded in two sections, the separate parts were joined together by a metal bridge over the nose. The Mk.IVa looked very similar to the Mk.IV and despite efforts to reduce weight, it was only half-an-ounce less. The split lens arrangement was maintained, as was the 'flip-shield'. A very limited number were produced and not many are known to have survived.

In time, the weight of the Mk.IVa and the complexity of its construction lead to some radical changes, but the Air Ministry persevered with the design which it considered was basically sound.

These Mk.IVA google are the rarest survivors of the Battle of Britain period and are therefore coveted by collectors. The Mk.IVA goggles were an attempt to produce a lighter version of the Mk.IV and these were constructed of Bakelite instead of brass. Only marginally lighter, they were not considered a success. They often became brittle and were therefore easily broken, hence they do not survive very well. (Mick Prodger Collection)

GOGGLES, FLYING, Mk.IVB
Stores Reference: 22C/167

This pair of goggles was designed around the best features of the Mk.IV and the Mk.IVa googles. Although they were still heavy brass, they were simpler in design and eliminated much of the fiddly construction of the earlier versions.

The Mk.IVb retained the flip-down lens, though these also proved unpopular and were often removed. It is believed that many pilots preferred to use the tinted lenses which were supplied with the goggles.

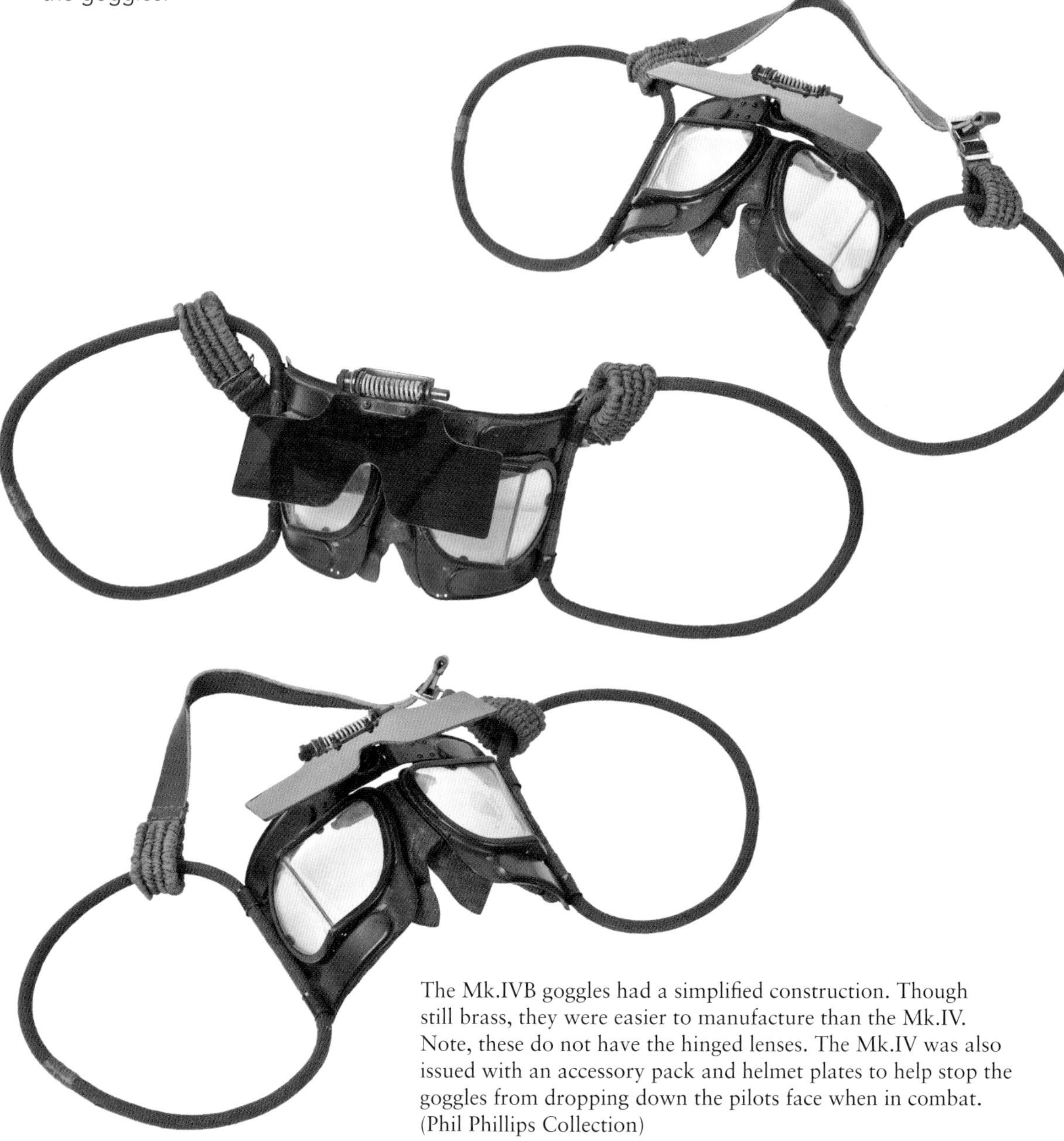

The Mk.IVB goggles had a simplified construction. Though still brass, they were easier to manufacture than the Mk.IV. Note, these do not have the hinged lenses. The Mk.IV was also issued with an accessory pack and helmet plates to help stop the goggles from dropping down the pilots face when in combat. (Phil Phillips Collection)

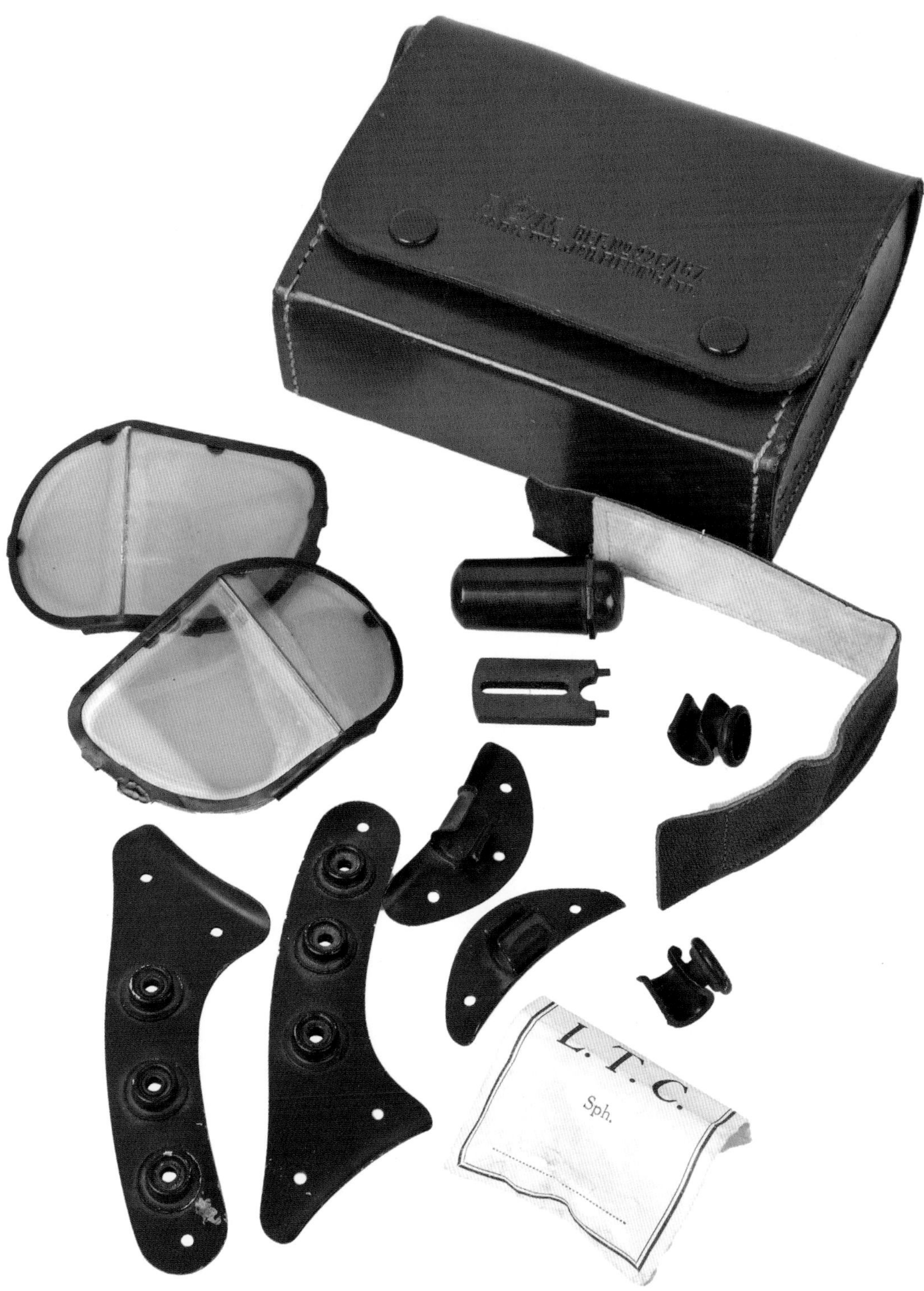

The accessory pack provided with the Mk.IVB goggles which included spare lenses and helmet plates to fit to the top of the B type flying helmet. (Phil Phillips Collection)

ABOVE: The leather case for the accessory pack for the Mk.IVB googles was stamped externally with the Air Ministry mark and the stores reference number. (Phil Phillips Collection)

BELOW: A box for a pair of Mk.IVB goggles. A rare survivor, it shows the stores reference number of 22c/167. (Phil Phillips Collection)

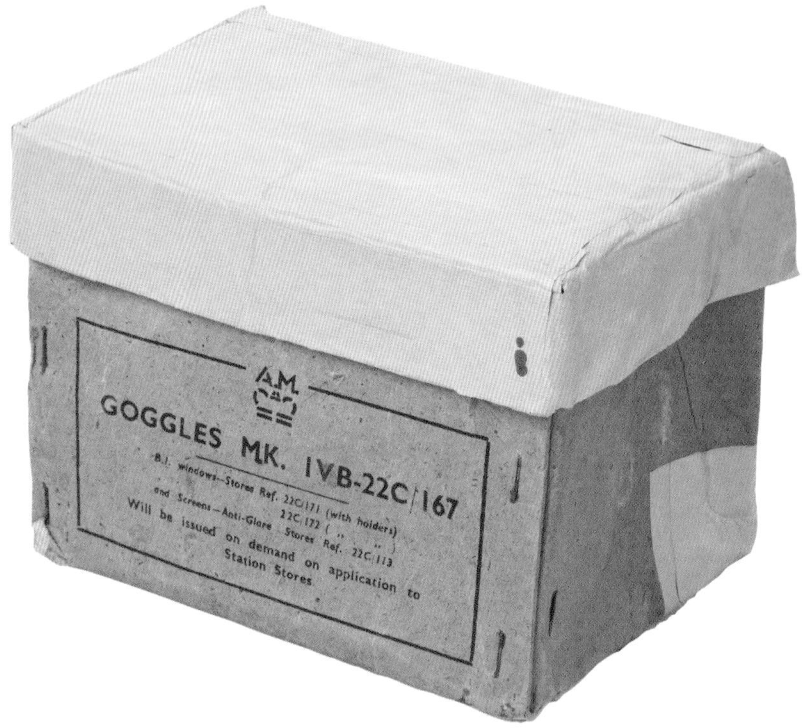

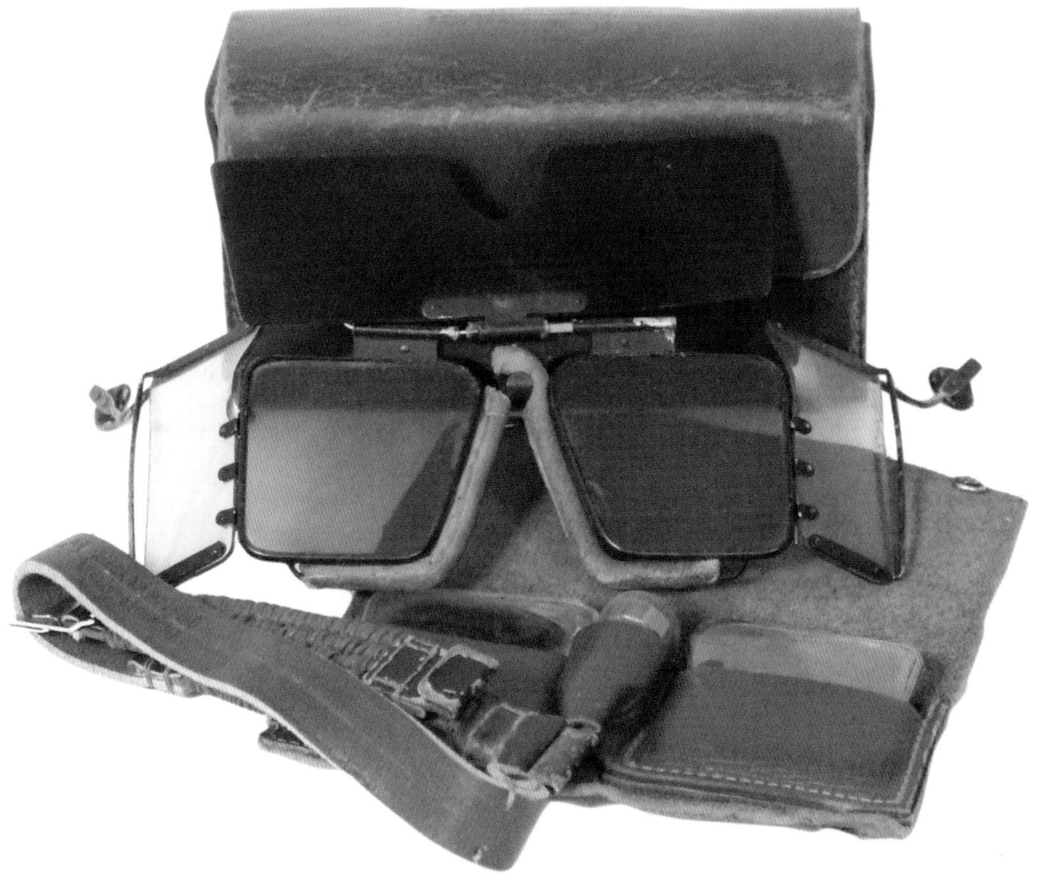

A very rare set of Mk.Va googles which were mainly associated with, and available to, Fleet Air Arm and Coastal Command personnel. (Simon Lannoy Collection)

GOGGLES, FLYING, Mk.VA
Stores Reference: 22C/156

These lightweight frame goggles, or glasses, have been included for completeness. Generally associated with use by Coastal Command during the early war years, they do appear in period photographs of fighter pilots in the Battle of Britain, a result of the transfer of pilots from Coastal Command and the Fleet Air Arm to Fighter Command.

The Mk.Va are of a lightweight frame construction with detachable strap. Both sides of the frame and flip shield are mounted on a thin metal hinge with a rolled rubber padding which protects the nose.

LUXOR GOGGLES
Private Purchase

Luxor goggles became identifiable with the Battle of Britain through the well-known photograph of Pilot Officer Keith Gillman which appeared on the cover of *Picture Post* Magazine at the end of

August 1940. As part of 'B' Flight, 32 Squadron, Gillman was photographed for the press at RAF Hawkinge on 29 July 1940. In the image used on *Picture Post*, he was wearing a pair of 'Luxor 12' goggles. Sadly, Gillman was lost on 25 August 1940, the magazine being published a week later.

As they were not approved by the Air Ministry, it is likely that Gillman was one a small number of pilots who opted to wear Luxor goggles during the Battle, the majority opting to remain with service issue designs.

Whilst similar brands of goggles can be seen in contemporary Battle of Britain images, it is the name of Luxor that has stuck. The Luxor goggles typically had teardrop-shaped lenses, adjustable bridge and vented eye pieces. With an elasticised strap, each half was a one-piece, flat triplex lens.

Such goggles were available pre-war at most flying clubs and there were numerous manufacturers in the UK, Europe, and the USA. They were used by motor racing drivers, motor cyclists' as well as private pilots. They were apparently much more comfortable and well-fitting than any of the Air Ministry designs, and, of course, lightweight.

ABOVE and RIGHT: A pair of Luxor 'Twelve' goggles made by E.B. Meyrovitz. These have the clear laminated lenses, which are teardrop in shape, and the vented eye pieces. These were available pre-war at most flying clubs and also for motor racing. (Phil Phillips Collection)

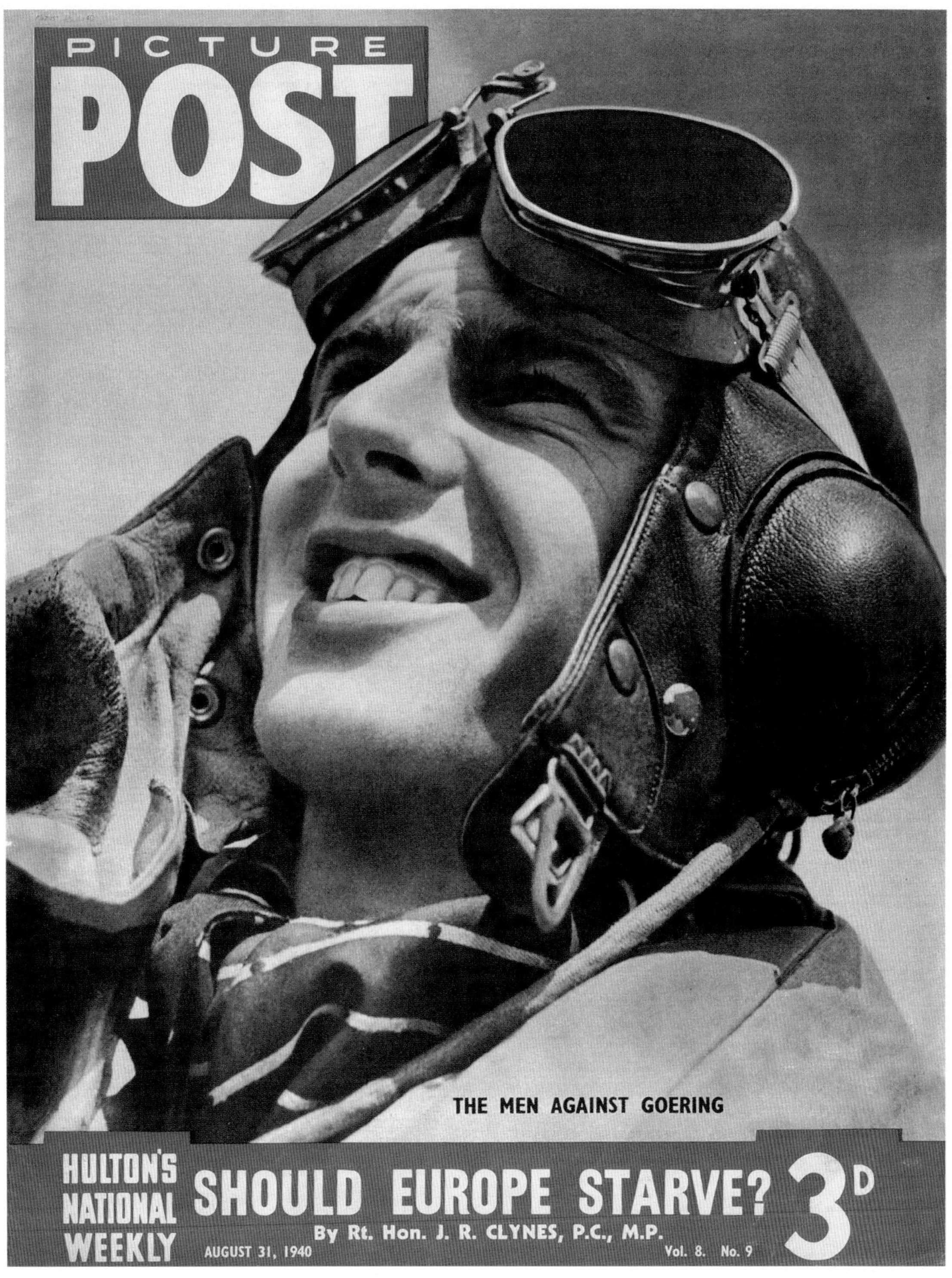

The front cover of *Picture Post* of 31 August 1940, showing Pilot Officer Keith Gillman wearing his Luxor 12 flying goggles. (Historic Military Press)

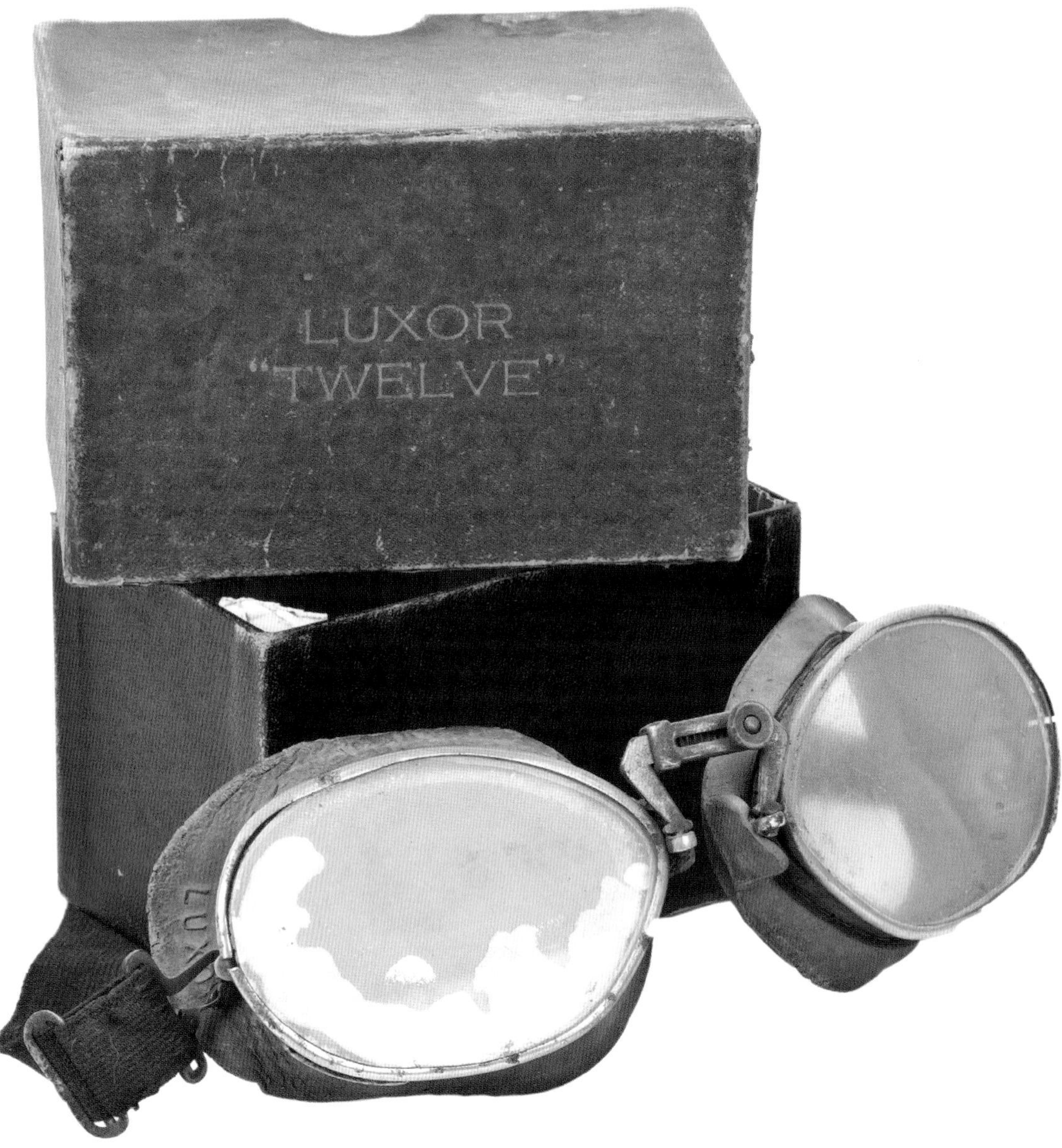

The Luxor 'Twelve' goggles with their original box. (Phil Phillips Collection)

Section 3
OXYGEN MASKS

OXYGEN MASK, D TYPE
Stores Reference: 6D/105

This mask is particularly rare and difficult to find today in good condition. As a design, it really dates back to the 1930s but was in use well into the war and was the mainstay for aircrew during the Battle of Britain period. It was designed as an oxygen mask, but could also be used as just a microphone carrier and during 1940 there were a number of variations seen.

At first glance, the mask has a green cloth exterior (wool barathea) which internally has a chamois leather lining, this being padded to help create a seal against the face of the wearer. It was secured to the B Type helmet with two snap fasteners each side of the mask and had a wire stiffener on the fabric to help shape around the nose. The mask was sewn to a brass ring, to which the oxygen inlet was fitted. The microphone, in turn, was then fitted to the end cap. The mask was issued with a further black lacquered metal end cap covered with a white chamois leather to the front; these could be used if no communication system was required.

The oxygen used reached the mask through a narrow rubber tube which, on early examples of the type, had a beige cloth wrapping externally to prevent freezing. This was later changed to and black and yellow fleck. The pipe fitted over the inlet tube on the metal ring on the right as you look at the mask and was bound tight into place with linen thread.

Squadron Leader Geoffrey Wellum DFC recalled checking his oxygen as he climbed through 9,000 feet – it was accepted that once over 10,000 feet you would generally need oxygen otherwise you would suffer from hypoxia and possibly pass out: 'I glance at the altimeter. It reads 9,250 feet or thereabouts. Turn on the oxygen, wouldn't do to forget that. Turn the tap to emergency and feel the flow inside the mask against my cheek.'[7]

The types of microphone used on D Type mask during the Battle of Britain were of two main designs. These hinged open from the ring to facilitate communication on the ground or, apparently, to enable the wearer to be sick! There was an E Type carbon microphone assembly which was a chamois-covered, bell-shaped affair mainly used by the Blenheim crews.

The Type 19 electro-magnetic microphone assembly, which came into service in January 1939, was mainly used by the fighter pilots as the Spitfire and Hurricane required UHF magnetic microphones. This assembly had a characteristic chamois covered flat front with a serrated disk switch on the side, although, due to the flimsy switch, it was not easy to operate during combat. Subsequently an Air

Ministry Order required that all switches were to be removed, so a true Battle of Britain microphone will have the switch removed.

A further variant was the Type 21 microphone. This was officially introduced into service on 3 October 1940, late on in the Battle of Britain.

The connector from the microphone cable to the aircraft was a jack-plug type male connector. If you baled out, the connection to the aircraft would, therefore, easily break.

ABOVE and OPPOSITE ABOVE: A D Type oxygen mask with the E Type microphone assembly, the latter being a chamois-covered bell-shaped affair mainly used by the Blenheim crews. It is shown being worn on a B Type flying helmet, which had the two female poppers to fix the mask too, with Luxor goggles. Note the oxygen supply coming out of the left-hand side of the assembly, as well as the male connector for the microphone and ear pieces. (Phil Phillips Collection)

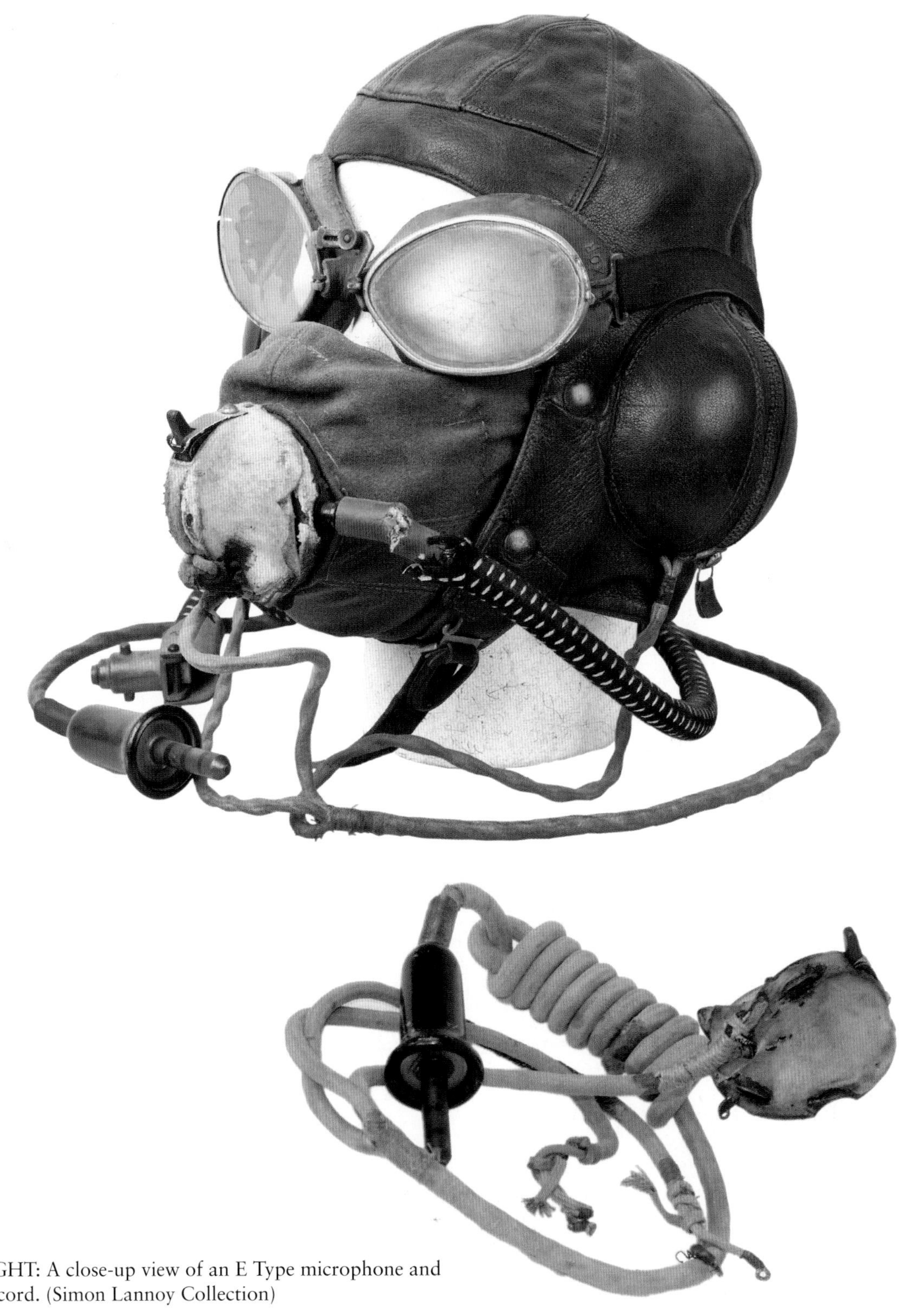

RIGHT: A close-up view of an E Type microphone and its cord. (Simon Lannoy Collection)

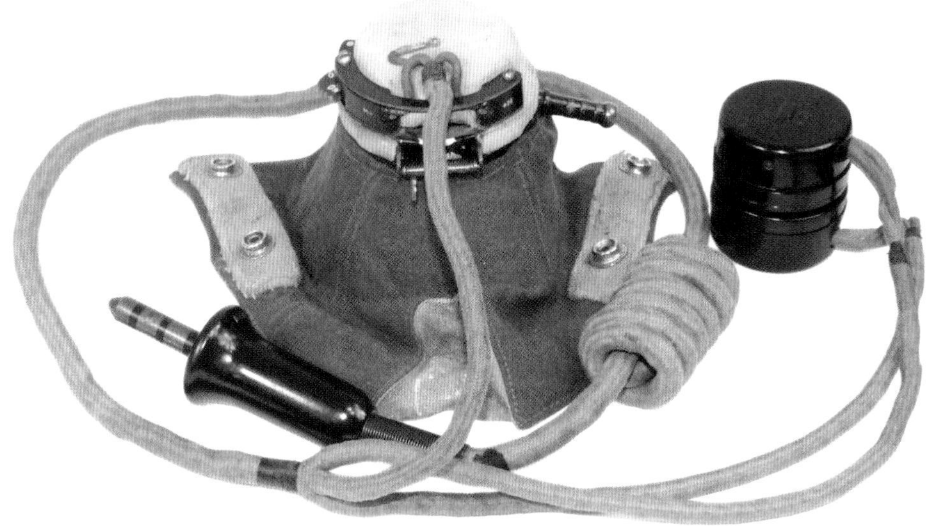

ABOVE and BELOW: An example of a D Type oxygen mask with the Type 19 magnetic microphone assembly used mainly by single-seat fighter pilots. Note the difference in the shape of the microphone assembly from that on the E Type. (Simon Lannoy Collection)

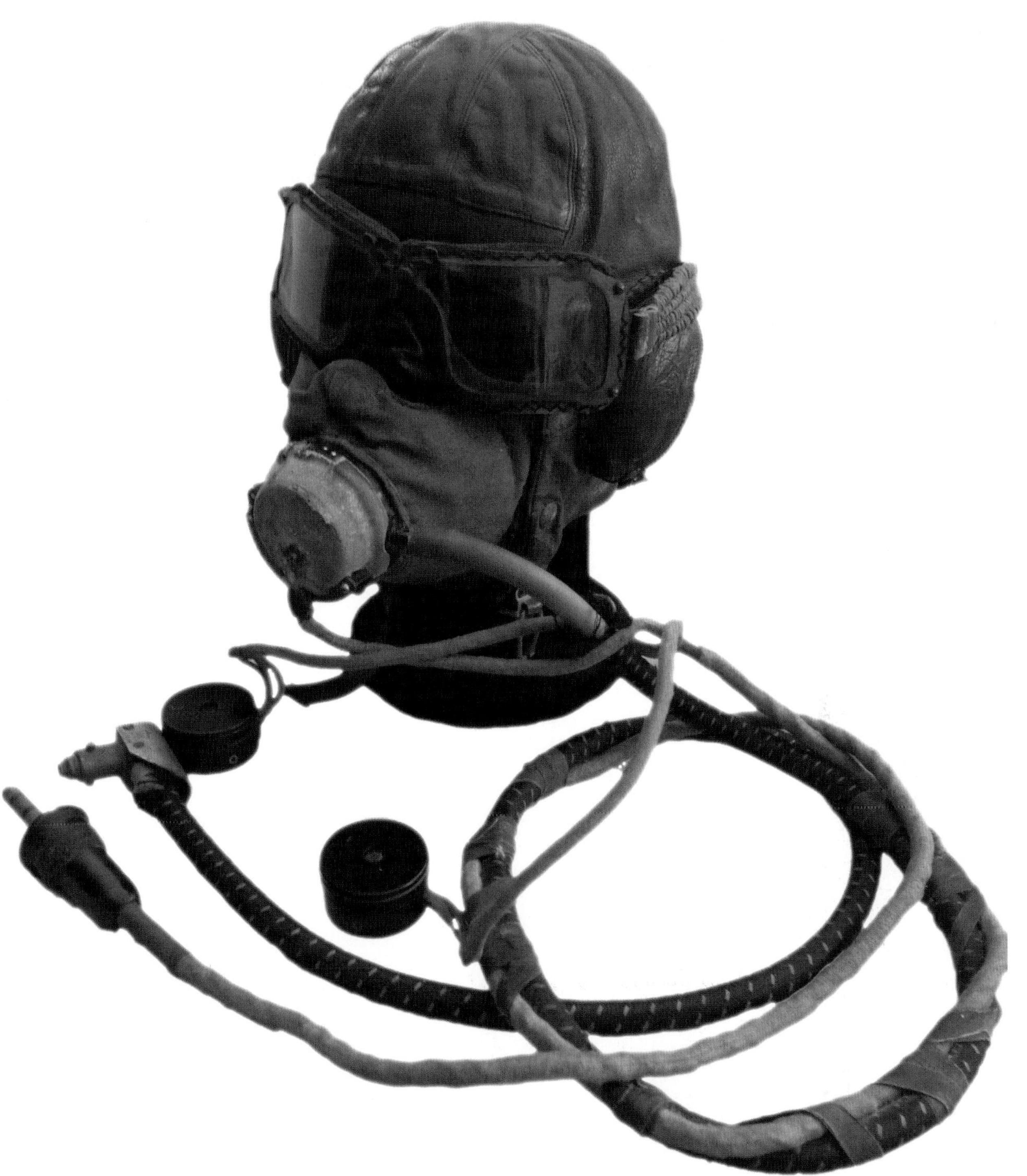

PREVIOUS PAGE: A classic Battle of Britain pilot's flying helmet set up. This B Type helmet is believed to have belonged to Sergeant Rudolf Zima, a Czech pilot who flew Hurricanes with 310 Squadron during the Battle of Britain, having joined the squadron (which was based at Duxford) in August 1940. The initials inside are 'RZ'.

The modifications made to the microphone and oxygen hose indicate a Battle of Britain time period. The kit includes Mk.IIIa goggles, a D Type mask made of green wool Barathea which is lined with chamois and fitted with a Type 19 Microphone. The latter is an extremely rare electro-magnetic microphone complete with wiring loom and plug. The Type 19 microphone is the 'flat-fronted' chamois-covered pattern that was introduced in January 1939 and used in conjunction with the D Type oxygen mask throughout the Battle of Britain. An 'on-off' switch, operated by a small serrated disc, was mounted within an assembly at the lower side of the microphone. An Air Ministry Order actually called for the removal of the serrated disc switch knob to prevent accidental turning off of the microphone. By October 1940, the Type 20/Type 21 assembly had been introduced.

As can be seen in the photograph the original oxygen tube is present, although when this was first connected to the mask it would have been whipped to prevent it being disconnected, the cord being lashed around the material to create a tight connection. However, many aircrew decided to cut back the fleck material covering to aid disconnection of the tube.

Note the early 'Gunfire' oxygen connector. The telephone receivers for the radio of the Type 7063 variant and fit into the ear cups. The covering for the wiring or armoured tubbing is of any early style; the user has taped the oxygen tube and radio leads together to stop them being caught up and tangled in the cockpit.

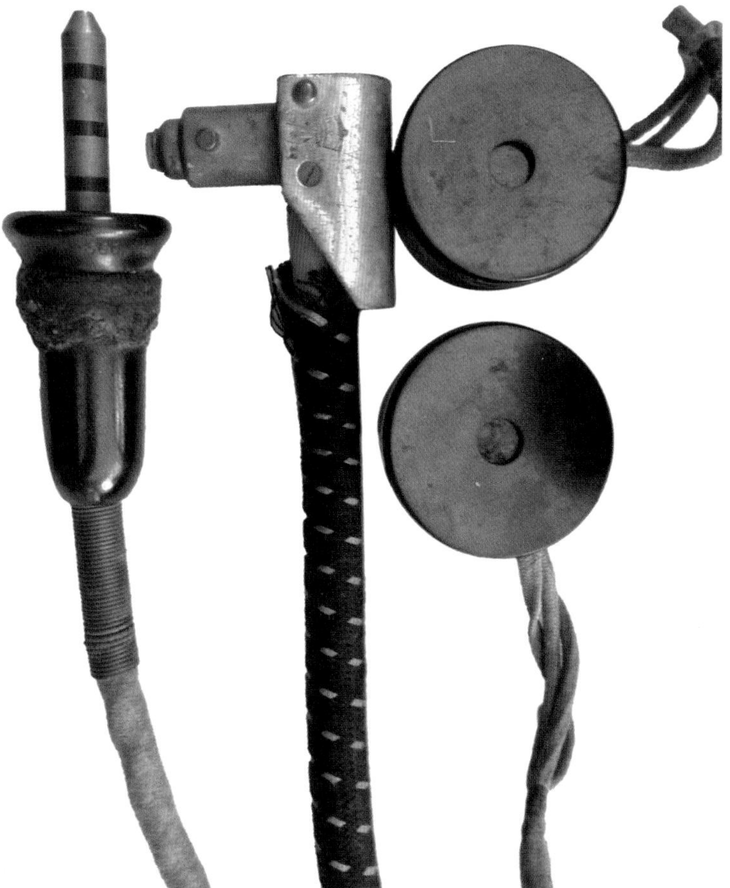

LEFT: Here we can see elements of the classic Battle of Britain pilot's flying helmet set up displayed on the previous page. From left to right these are the Bakelite radio jack, the brass 'Gunfire' oxygen connector (the Air Ministry markings can be seen; 'Gunfire' is stamped on the reverse), and two telephone receivers.

Section 4
FLYING CLOTHING

Until the introduction of enclosed cockpit fighters such as the Gloster Gladiator, Hawker Hurricane and Supermarine Spitfire, one of the biggest problems facing the fighter pilot was the extreme cold at altitude, not just the outside air temperature but also the wind chill factor from the wind around the cockpit. This necessitated the use of bulky flying suits and gloves which were not really ideal for the more modern aircraft.

Although the cockpits of the Spitfire and Hurricane were not heated, they were considerably warmer than their predecessors, the cockpit canopy not only giving a degree of protection but also acting as a greenhouse in the summer months. That said, at altitude, the same problem of cold still prevailed and required some clothing protection. Most of the pre-war equipment was of reverse sheepskin construction and very little was actually leather.

At the start of 1940 pilots were still being issued with the bulky Sidcot suit, although most preferred to leave this piece of kit behind and opted for flying in dress uniform and, if necessary, wear an Irvin jacket on top.

Flying Officer Harold Bird-Wilson, of 17 Squadron, remembered what he wore during that period: 'We flew in ordinary uniforms. We had no overalls in those days. We had jolly good sheepskin lined flying boots, leather gloves and helmets. We had sheepskin leather jackets and Mae Wests'.[8]

Some pilots even flew with just their pyjamas on, as Bird-Wilson continued: 'We sometimes used to sleep at our dispersal points. Some pilots actually scrambled and flew in their pyjamas.'[9]

Wing Commander Tom Neil DFC & Bar, AFC, AE, once recalled the options available to pilots during the summer of 1940: 'If the squadron was at readiness immediately, it also meant getting out of bed, dressing and donning flying clothing, or putting a Sidcot suit or Irving jacket – the ubiquitous 'goon-skin'- over pyjamas.'[10]

Some opted for using the white or black 'Prestige' one-piece flying suits issued to pre-war aerobatic teams or also available as a private purchase item.

The pilots soon found that the shirt and tie combination of the service dress was not ideal in combat, as during a patrol or engagement they needed to move their head about to keep a good look out and ensure no enemy aircraft were in their six o'clock position. Also, if you were unlucky enough to be shot down or suffer engine failure over the English Channel, the collar of your standard officer's Van Heusen shirt 'shrank in contact with sea water and throttled the wearer'. Many pilots, therefore, soon abandoned the tie and opted for a silk scarf around the open neck. This also stopped chaffing whilst a pilot was keeping a good look out, as remembered by Sergeant Cyril 'Bam' Bamberger of

Nos.41 and 610 squadrons: 'I always flew with a silk scarf round my neck so that I had the freedom to turn my neck through 360 degrees.'[11]

Rather than the issue shirts with detachable collars, another option for pilots was a 'white aircrew frock', essentially a woollen crew-neck sweater which was commonly an off-white colour. Some pilots wore home knitted jumpers under their service dress, normally black or white.

Although officers were expected to purchase their own personal equipment from a tailor, all flying clothing was issued as what was termed 'public clothing', i.e. at the public expense, as Air Publication 958 states: 'An officer of the general duties branch up to and including the rank of wing commander, who is fit for flying duties, will be in possession of a complete set of flying clothing. He may however, provide himself with articles of private flying clothing in lieu of similar articles of service pattern if he prefers to do so and his C.O considers the private articles satisfactory'.[12]

Such rules gave pilots the opportunity to purchase private flying suits if desired. However, some individuals, such as Squadron Leader Brian Lane DFC of 19 Squadron, went one step further. In period photographs, he can be seen in what appears to be a battledress tunic. However, as these items, which came be officially known as Suits, Aircrew, Blouse, were not formal issue until 1941, it is thought that Lane is actually wearing a 'prestige' type flying suit cut down and adapted for use under his 'Mae West'. The Army had been wearing battledress uniform from the start of the war and it is thought that he may have copied this style. It certainly would have been more comfortable for wear in the cockpit than the service dress.

A group of pilots of 303 Squadron pictured at RAF Leconfield after returning from a fighter sortie, 24 October 1940. The Hurricane in the background is Mk.I V6684, coded RF-F. From left to right, in the front row, are: Pilot Officer Mirosław Ferić; Flight Lieutenant John A. Kent (the CO of 'A' Flight); Flying Officer Bogdan Grzeszczak; Pilot Officer Jerzy Radomski; Pilot Officer Witold Łokuciewski; Pilot Officer Bogusław Mierzwa (obscured by Łokuciewski); Flying Officer Zdzisław Henneberg; Sergeant Jan Rogowski; and Sergeant Eugeniusz Szaposznikow. In the centre, to the rear of this group, wearing helmet and goggles, is Pilot Officer Jan Zumbach. The majority of these men are wearing 32 Pattern life preservers and Irvin jackets. (Polish Institute and Sikorski Museum London)

ABOVE: A Battle of Britain Blenheim pilot wearing a B Type helmet with Mk.IIIa googles and Irvin jacket. (Mark Hillier Collection)

BELOW: Members of a Battle of Britain Blenheim crew pose for the camera. The radio operator in the pilot's seat is wearing a B Type helmet with Mk.IIIa googles. (Mark Hillier Collection)

THERMALLY INSULATED FLYING SUIT (IRVIN SUIT) JACKET
Stores Reference: 22C/98

One of the most iconic items of flying clothing from the Battle of Britain period is, of course, the Irvin jacket. Issued to all aircrew, they are seen in many of the press photographs and newsreels of the time, though were not often worn for combat.

Originally manufactured by the Irvin parachute company, the Irvin jacket, as they were commonly known, would subsequently be manufactured by many other companies. The jacket had been designed by Leslie Irvin in the 1930s and was initially produced in a factory at Letchworth, Hertfordshire. It is thought that the earliest Air Ministry-issue examples were available from 1932 onwards.

Though the jacket had been designed with the intention of using the supplest material possible, to help pilots move freely in the cockpit, the Irvin jacket was still very bulky. It was constructed from thick pile sheepskin with the outer being dyed brown. The collar could be turned up and had an elastic strap fitting in to two eyelets to help it stand up in the slipstream of an open cockpit aircraft. The zips to the front and cuffs were marked with 'Made in England', with 'Dot' in the centre of a circle, each zip having a leather tag.

The early variants had a single seam down the back as materials were plentiful. Later on in the war the back was more commonly constructed from four panels. The jacket was provided with a leather belt around the waist which was not included on the earliest models in the 1930s.

ABOVE and LEFT: The iconic Irvin jacket, available from the early 1930s, the jacket being part of a full suit. The jacket can frequently be seen being worn by fighter pilots in photographs taken during the Battle of Britain, but rarely the trousers. Of note is the single seam down the rear of the jacket which identifies it as an early example, the later versions having a two-seam rear of four panels. Note the elastic strap at the rear of the hood. (Phil Phillips Collection)

THERMALLY INSULATED FLYING SUIT (IRVIN SUIT) TROUSERS
Stores Reference: 22C/99

The trousers that went to make up the full Irvin Suit were constructed from the same material as the jacket. As with the jacket the trousers, though available, were not often worn by fighter pilots. They were extremely heavy and were supported by a pair of internal braces.

The trousers were zipped from top to bottom for ease of access and to assist when treating wounds, this being the same type of zip used on the jacket. The trousers had two pockets on the legs.

An example of the Irvin suit's thermally insulated trousers which were issued with the jacket. These were made from the same materials as the jacket. The braces were required to support them whilst being worn due to their weight. Not often worn by the fighter pilots, they were commonly used by the crews of Bomber and Coastal commands. (Phil Phillips Collection)

A group shot of 249 Squadron pilots taken during September 1940 at North Weald. From left to right, they are: Pilot Officer Percival R.F. Burton, Flight Lieutenant Robert Barton, Flight Lieutenant Albert Lewis DFC (wearing 1939 Pattern boots), Pilot Officer James Crossey, Flight Lieutenant Tom Neil, Pilot Officer John Beazley, Squadron Leader John Grandy, Pilot Officer George Barclay and Flight Lieutenant Keith Lofts. Behind them is a 249 Squadron Hurricane, although it still bears the squadron code (US) as worn by 56 Squadron. On arrival at North Weald, 249 Squadron took over the Hurricanes of 56 Squadron and it was some time before the US codes were replaced with 249's GN code. This iconic photograph became one of the best-known images of the Battle of Britain, especially after it featured in the 1941 Air Ministry (HMSO) publication on the Battle of Britain. (Andy Saunders Collection)

1930 PATTERN, FLYING SUIT 'SIDCOT'
Stores Reference: 22C/54

This was a one-piece flying suit, the design of which was based on a Sidcot suit used in the First World War.

The 1930 Pattern example was constructed of lightweight waterproof green cotton which was lined with linen. It had a large, flapped collar and a further thick pile fleece collar could be buttoned to it. It featured a map pocket on the left breast and two larger fleece-lined pockets on each leg. It was bulky enough to be worn over uniform, or could be used on its own as it had a range of button in linings that could be utilised. One of these was known as the Fur Fabric Liner (Teddy Bear Suit). With the stores reference 22C/53, this was a one-piece brown simulated fur fabric liner which buttoned into the Sidcot. Alternatively, there was a quilted kapok liner. With the stores reference 22C/301-309, this was introduced in 1940.

Flight Lieutenant Jimmy Corbin DFC, a sergeant pilot at the time, remembered his initial flying kit issue during his flying training in 1939: 'I was issued with my leather helmet and green-grey Sidcot flying suit as well as goggles, gloves and gauntlets similar to those used by motorcycle riders.'[13]

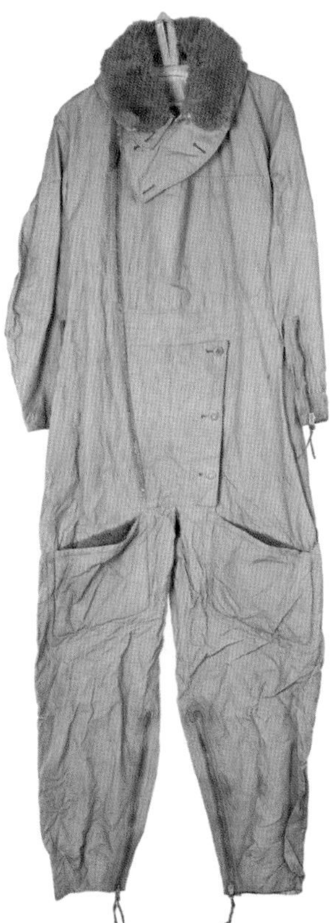

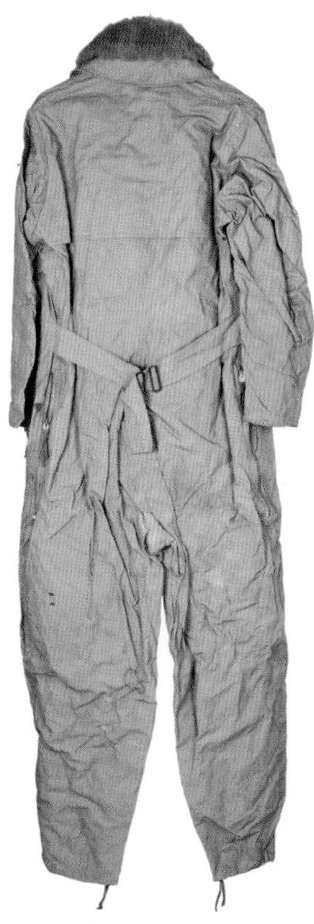

The 1930 Pattern 'Sidcot' flying suit seen here with its detachable fur lined collar which was buttoned on to the suit. This is just the outer and a lined inner suit can also be worn for extra protection. Note the two fur lined pockets on the front of the legs and the diagonal zip on the upper body to aid access. The arm pits were vented and the suit is also provided with a belt. (Phil Phillips Collection)

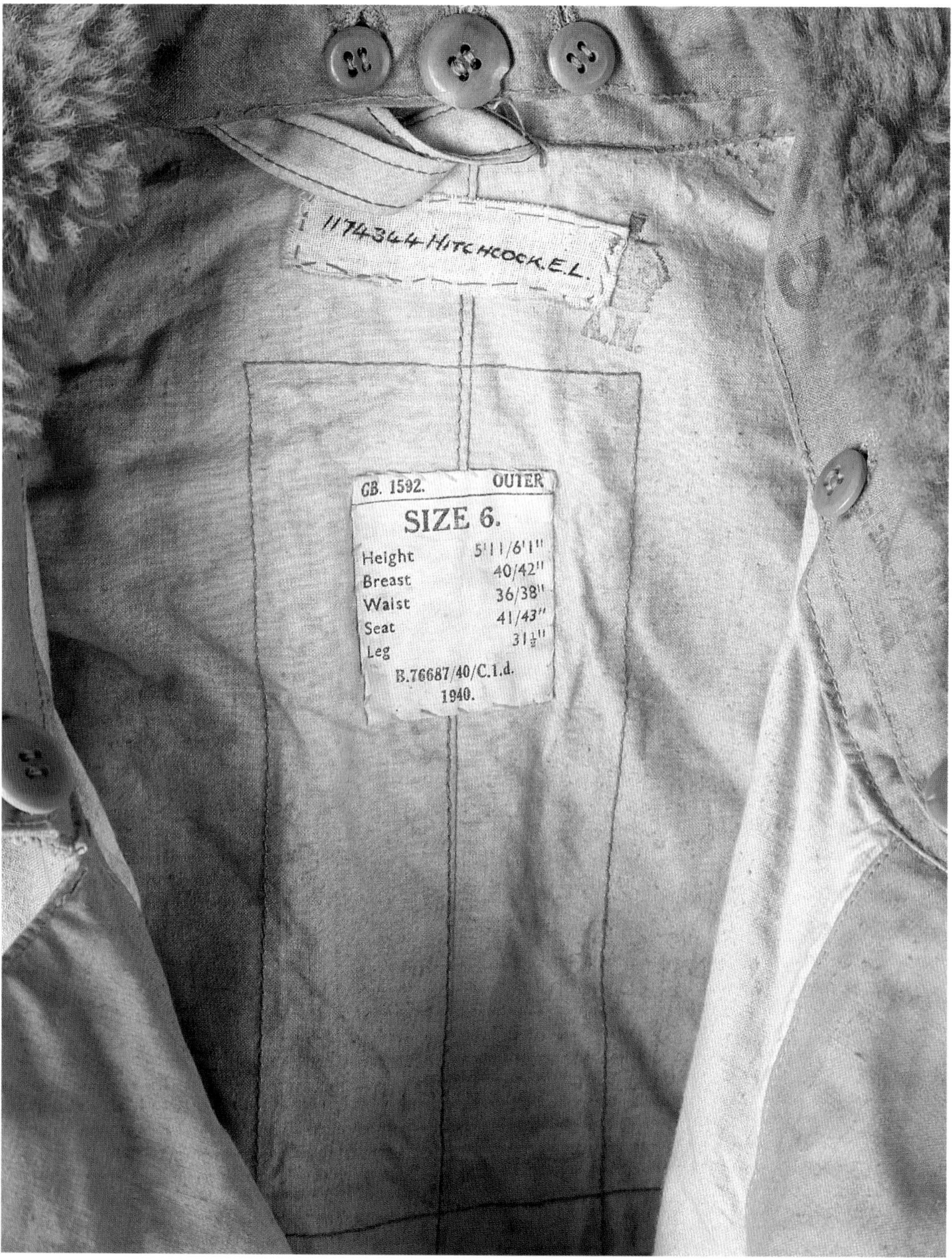

A close-up of the Air Ministry stamps visible to the collar of the Sidcot Suit and also the labelling within showing the 1940 date. (Phil Phillips Collection)

Squadron Leader Douglas Bader (centre) pictured wearing a 1930 Pattern flying suit, often called a Sidcot Suit, whilst serving with 242 Squadron during the Battle of Britain. Bader liked to use the suit as he could keep his artificial legs installed in one, ready to scramble. The other two pilots are sporting examples of the 'Prestige' flying suit. (Mark Hillier Collection)

WHITE COTTON UNLINED FLYING SUIT
Stores Reference: 22C

These issue suits were originally intended for pilots who had a prestigious position in one of the pre-war aerobatic display teams or who were to participate in flying displays such as those at Hendon. Nevertheless, they continued to be used throughout the Battle of Britain by some of the pilots. Many more pilots also had private purchase examples, which could be obtained in black or white, to go over their expensive, tailored uniforms. It would appear that the latter pilots were mainly from Auxiliary Air Force squadrons.

These suits could also be purchased in heavy dark blue or black cotton, these private purchase suits could be obtained through outfitters such as Gieves or Selfridges. Some photographs show that the squadron crest was often sewn on to the left breast, but this practice was halted on security grounds during the Battle of Britain.

One of the most well-known wearers of such clothing was Air Vice Marshal Keith Park, a New Zealander who commanded No.11 Group. During the Battle of Britain, he was often seen visiting his units wearing a white flying suit in his personal Hurricane. Likewise, in many staged images of 242 Squadron, it appears that some of its pilots wore examples of the 'prestige' flying suit.

ABOVE: A white cotton example of the private purchase 'Prestige' suit. Note the leg map pockets low on the legs and the V-shaped collar. The belt is a single row of holes to fasten the buckle rather than a double on the issue. (Phil Phillips Collection)

LEFT: This is the white cotton Unlined Flying Suit (Stores Reference 22C) which issued to pre-war aerobatic teams who flew at the RAF Hendon Air Display and other such events. This issue suit is white cotton and has four pockets closed with RAF Brass buttons, note the leg pockets are much higher up than on the private purchase 'Prestige' suit. The suit is belted at the waist. This suit has rank tabs, again buttoned, this example showing the rank of Group Captain. (Phil Phillips Collection)

A group of personnel of 242 (Canadian) Squadron pictured at Duxford during 1940. The Commanding Officer, Squadron Leader Douglas Bader DSO (front centre), is wearing his 1930 Pattern flying suit, commonly known as the Sidcot Suit, whilst the majority of the others are again wearing examples of the 'Prestige' flying suit. (Historic Military Press)

A black cotton example of the same private purchase suit. This one carries the squadron badge of 79 Squadron. During the Battle of Britain, the Air Ministry issued orders for these badges to be removed. (Phil Phillips Collection)

Wearing a 'Prestige' flying suit, 145 Squadron's Flight Lieutenant Adrian Hope Boyd inspects German ammunition during a period of rest outside 'B' Flight's hut at RAF Westhampnett. Eric Marsden, one of the groundcrew who looked after Boyd's Hurricane during the Battle of Britain, remembers that Boyd had a fixation with German ammunition and would often take it apart or, if he could not dismantle it, saw it in half. (Andy Saunders Collection)

Pilot Officer A.V. 'Taffy' Clowes of No.1 Squadron RAF standing by the nose of his Hawker Hurricane Mk.I, P3395 'JX-B', at Wittering, Huntingdonshire. The wasp emblem was painted on the nose of his aircraft during the Battle of Britain. Clowes is wearing a B Type flying helmet with a white 'prestige' flying suit with white opera scarf. (Andy Saunders Collection)

PILOTS' SCARVES

These were never an issue item and many of those seen in period images were actually made by Tootal, although there were other manufacturers. They are elongated (rather than square) and usually have a silk side for appearance and a wool side for warmth, although a number are double-ply silk.

An example of the private purchase silk opera style scarf. Pilots would wear these inside the uniform jacket to help prevent chafing from the stiff shirt collar material. (Simon Lannoy Collection)

The silk (later examples used a Rayon mix) is very substantial – the sort of silk used for jacket linings would be the best comparison. The typical patterns seen worn by many pilots and aircrew are university or school stripes, Paisley pattern or small polka-dots. White scarves worn in 1940 were usually opera scarves. They were also made of substantial silk with a seamed, double-sided construction.

The pilots often removed the collars of their shirts as they were too rough by some, causing friction when looking out for enemy aircraft. This could lead to a rash developing on a pilot's neck, as recalled by Wing Commander Bob Doe DSO, DFC & Bar: 'I flew in uniform trousers and shoes, uniform shirt and jacket, and after the first painful experience, no collar, but a silk scarf. Some of the chaps wore a silk stocking but that was, I thought, a little ostentatious.'[14]

The King's Regulations covered the matter of scarves and fur collars, stating that 'an officer or airman is forbidden to wear a scarf of any description with uniform, except while in the air'.[15] From photographs, however, it seems that this order was ignored whilst pilots were at dispersal or on readiness.

FROCK, WHITE, AIRCREW
Stores Reference: 22G/63

This item was a knitted high-neck sweater in cream or off-white wool, but can also found in black. It was worn under the service dress or flying clothing for extra warmth.

Regularly seen being worn by pilots during the Battle of Britain, this piece of clothing was only authorised for wear during combat duty as long as they did not show. Some images show slight variations and colours and it is likely that they were home-knitted, which *The King's Regulations* permitted. Again, this would have been softer round the neck rather than the chaffing by the starched shirt collar.

ABOVE and RIGHT: The issue white aircrew frock often seen worn under a uniform jacket. These were also found in black, though such examples more likely to be knitted by families or privately purchased. (Simon Lannoy Collection)

Pilot Officer Archibald Lyall pictured at Westhampnett during the Battle of Britain, at which point he was flying with 602 (City of Glasgow) Squadron. He is wearing what appears to be an issue white aircrew frock, over which is his 1937 Pattern life-preserver. During his time at the West Sussex airfield, Lyall achieved a number of kills, his tally eventually amounting to three destroyed, three shared, two probable, five damaged and four shared damaged. He was shot down over the Isle of Wight on 28 November 1940, but baled out too low from Spitfire N3242. He died aged 27 and was cremated at Woodvale Crematorium, Brighton. (Andy Saunders Collection)

Undoubtedly a staged photograph, the pilot in this picture is wearing a white Prestige flying suit, woollen knitted gloves, a B Type leather flying helmet and D Type oxygen mask. Note also the private purchase Luxor style goggles which many pilots chose over the issue Mk.IIIa goggles, and the addition of a strap from a pair of either a Mk.III or Mk.IIIa googles, this being an unofficial alteration. Many pilots chose to fly in service dress and Mae West, so this is an unusual image and may date from early in the Battle of Britain. (Historic Military Press)

Section 5
FLYING BOOTS AND FOOTWEAR

It is not unusual to see groups of Battle of Britain pilots can be seen wearing a mix of flying equipment in period photographs, included when it comes to flying boots.

The earlier 1936 Pattern boot, of black leather fleece-lined manufacture, was replaced by the 1939 Pattern design. The latter had a fleece-lined canvas top section and black leather bottoms. Both types were worn during the Battle of Britain, though some pilots felt they were too cumbersome and heavy, and opted to fly in their service shoes instead as these, they felt, gave a greater 'feel' to the rudder and enabled more accurate flying. The only issue with wearing shoes being that a greater number of pilots suffered burns around the ankle. That said, statistics quoted for burn injuries in 1940 reveal ninety-one cases for the shin, ankle and foot, out of a total of 378 burn injuries, or 24% of the recorded burns, with the highest being lower arm and hand at ninety-seven cases.

Though flying boots gave greater protection in a burning aircraft, they were prone to coming off when trying to abandon a stricken aircraft. The other reason for choosing shoes may have been that it was easier to walk in them than boots if they were forced to bale out and had to make their way to civilisation.

There are some photographs taken in the summer of 1940 that also show some pilots still wearing the old 1930 Pattern boot which had long been superseded. These have not been included within the following descriptions, only the main issue types available.

1936 PATTERN FLYING BOOTS
Stores Reference: 22C/80

These sturdy pull-on boots, made of chromed black leather and lined with thick pile fleece, were the foot wear of choice for many during the Battle of Britain.

Constructed with a leather sole and rubber heel, the 1936 Pattern had leather pullers sewn inside the top of the boot to help get them on, there was also a leather tightening strap across the front of the boot which helped keep them in place when baling out.

ABOVE RIGHT: The all black leather, fleece-lined 1936 Pattern flying boot was still in widespread use during the Battle of Britain. The difference between the private purchase boots and the issue variety being that the latter were smooth leather rather than a pebble finish. (Phil Philips Collection)

INSET: The leather label inside a 1936 Pattern flying boot showing the Air Ministry marking and size information. (Simon Lannoy Collection)

A group photograph of 602 (City of Glasgow) Squadron personnel taken outside the Officers' Mess at Westhampnett in 1940. The pilot seated front left, Flight Lieutenant Christopher 'Micky' Mount, is wearing 1939 Pattern flying boots, whilst the man standing far right, Pilot Officer Glen 'Nuts' Niven, is wearing the earlier 1936 Pattern flying boot. Squadron Leader Sandy Johnstone is in the middle of the front row. The two squadron dogs are 'Crash', the Alsatian, and 'Belinda', who is being held by Pilot Officer Paddy Barthropp. Paddy joined the squadron in mid-September 1940, which helps dates the picture. (The 602 (City of Glasgow) Squadron Museum)

1939 PATTERN FLYING BOOTS
Stores Reference: 22C/225-233

These were extensively used during 1940, having been introduced into service on 22 February the same year. They were constructed to exactly the same pattern as the 1936 Pattern boots, but differed in that they had a green, vulcanized canvas upper which was not that successful as a waterproofing. It would soak up moisture and freeze at altitude.

There were in fact two versions of this pattern. The first had a webbing top strap on the boots, the second a leather strap. Whilst there is some disagreement about which of the two versions is the earlier one, both are correct for the period of the Battle of Britain.

ABOVE and RIGHT: The 1939 Pattern flying boot. It is the vulcanised canvas uppers that differentiate this type from the earlier 1936 Pattern. Although essentially the same style, they basically used different materials. (Simon Lannoy Collection)

1940 PATTERN FLYING BOOTS
Stores Reference: 22C/435-442

The RAF's 1940 Pattern issue flying boots were a reversion back to the much earlier 1930 style boot. Whilst it is thought that this type was not available during the Battle of Britain, as an exact date of the first issue cannot be confirmed it has been included here for reference.

In a departure from previous designs, the 1940 Pattern boots were generously cut and fitted with frontal zips, enabling clothing to be tucked into them. However, the disadvantage of this was soon found in that those forced to bale out often complained that their boots tended to fall away during the descent as they were too loose. A subsequent modification involved the addition of a single leather strap around the base of the ankles, which became the later 1941 Pattern flying boots.

Section 6
GLOVES

An essential piece of flying equipment was protection for the hands. To this end the RAF issued suitable protection from the multiple layers of glove. First, silk liners next to the skin, then the leather elbow length gauntlets which, although adequate protection against fire, still provided limited protection from the cold at altitude. Later on, in 1941, knitted fingerless gloves that could be worn over the liners, chamois liners were not available till after the Battle. The other reason that this combination of gloves was not used is that pilots again felt that the ensemble was all too clumsy and they could not 'feel' the aircraft.

Many pilots often only flew with the liners or with no gloves at all so they could get a better 'feel' for the controls. Wing Commander Thomas Neil of 249 Squadron, however, religiously always wore his goggles and gloves for a reason: 'I always wore goggles and gloves. The Hurricane got to within two to three thousand degrees centigrade in a matter of seconds after being set on fire and that's why so many people were terribly burned. When I'd first gone into action, I wore short sleeves and no goggles, but I soon changed that, believe you me'.

Indeed, South African Squadron Leader Pat Wells was also grateful for the protection offered by his gloves. They 'saved my hands from the fire', he once recalled, 'with skin hanging down in sheets from the face and legs I was taken to Leeds Castle Emergency Hospital'.

1933 PATTERN FLYING GAUNTLETS
Stores Reference: 22C/60 LEFT HAND, 22C/61 RIGHT HAND

These gauntlets, introduced into RAF service in 1933, were in use for most of the Second World War, and are the ones most commonly used by Battle of Britain aircrew.

Constructed from soft chestnut brown leather, they also had a zipper, for ease of use, running from the wrist to the cuff. These were also issued with the liners which made up the whole system, but they could all be worn separately, and, indeed, often were.

A pair of 1933 Pattern gauntlets, a throwback to the days of flying open cockpit. Leather with a zipper down to the cuff, these could be worn with silk liners but were not ideal for helping pilots 'feel' the aircraft. Many pilots opted not to wear them but suffered the consequences of horrific burns if shot down. (Phil Philips Collection)

INNER GLOVES, SILK
Stores Reference: 22C/9

To complement the flying gauntlets, and to ensure the pilots had enough protection from the elements at altitude, Inner Gloves, Silk were also issued. These were worn first with the leather gauntlets over the top. As there would naturally not have been a lot of sensitivity for operating controls when wearing all layers, many pilots opted for often just the silk liners.

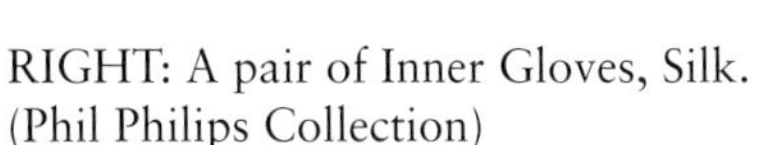

RIGHT: A pair of Inner Gloves, Silk. (Phil Philips Collection)

BELOW: The 1933 Pattern gauntlets along with the Inner Gloves, Silk and, laying on top, some chamois leather liners. The later which were issued after the Battle of Britain, but are shown here to provide an illustration of the layering that could be used with the gauntlets. (Phil Phillips Collection)

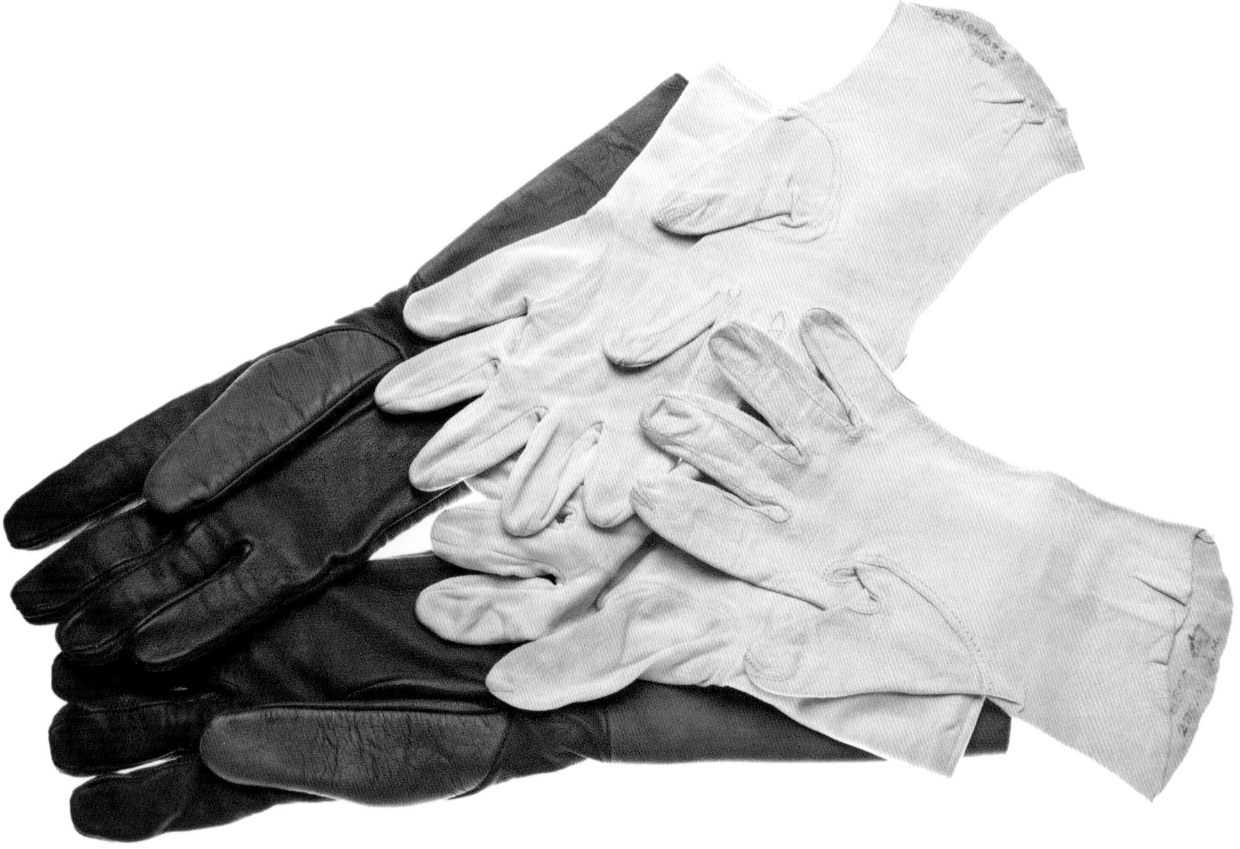

Section 7
LIFESAVING EQUIPMENT

During the early months of the Second World War little thought went into the development and use of lifesaving equipment, apart from the parachute and life-preserver. The experiences of the Battle of Britain, however, provided an impetus for change.

In terms of those items that were issued, *The King's Regulations* dated 1940 gave rules for officers and airmen alike. Regulation 705A stated: 'Lifesaving waistcoats of an approved pattern will invariably be carried for every occupant of an aircraft flying over water.'

The orders continue identifying the need of each squadron commanding officer to carry out 'periodical tests' to satisfy himself that all lifesaving waistcoats held on charge were fit for use. With regards parachutes, the regulations make it quite clear that each unit will have a parachute officer and that he will be responsible for the 'safe custody, maintenance and care' of the parachutes and ensure that the necessary training took place. Order 781 went on to state: 'All occupants of aircraft in which facilities are afforded for the use of parachutes will wear a parachute harness at all times when flying.'

In an emergency, some pilots struggled to get out of their aircraft, even those with sliding canopies, fighting against the slipstream and 'G' forces encountered once the aircraft started to go out of control. The problems faced by Bristol Blenheim night fighter crews when abandoning their aircraft whilst wearing a bulky parachute, due the size of the escape hatch, were described by Wing Commander Paul Le Rougetel DFC of 600 (City of London) Squadron:

'To extend the powered glide I had trimmed the Blenheim into a gentle turning descent with port power on. I moved to the hatch, leaned forward and groped for the latches. On pulling the hatch into the cockpit an unexpectedly strong rush of air forced my arms, holding the hatch, upwards and sideways.

'Twisting to get rid of the hatch to the rear, I tripped and fell heavily backwards in a sitting position, ending up with mu parachute pack jammed into the opening, while my legs and arms were inside the cabin. Eventually I discovered I could reach halfway up the back of the control column. By leaning forwards and pushing on it I was able to reduce speed and overcome the suction effect. I could then wriggle back into the cabin, put my legs through the escape hatch and fall through.'[16]

For many pilots in the Battle of Britain the parachute and life-preserver were often vital. That said, the latter was found to not always be ideal in rough seas and often needed to be topped up by mouth.

The colour of the life-preserver issued at the time was a sea grey/green colour which was not ideal for picking out pilots in the water either from the air or sea. At this stage, RAF fighter aircraft did not carry life rafts and there were no survival rations for pilots who were in the sea for a prolonged period.

For those who were shot down or suffered engine failure, the majority of aircrew either ended up in the sea or parachuting out. Once in the sea, those who were improperly dressed and difficult to spot may have suffered from exposure and the cold, possibly leading to hypothermia. Air Sea Rescue was at this stage of the war very primitive and items such as colourings to the life-preserver, aircrew whistles, dinghies and the like did not appear until later in the war.

Necessity being the mother of invention, the losses suffered and lessons learnt during the Battle of Britain prompted changes in early 1941. This section looks at the basic kit that a fighter pilot would have been issued with in the summer of 1940.

WAISTCOAT, LIFESAVING, STOLE PATTERN, TEMPERATE
Stores Reference: 22C/55

This item was introduced in 1932 and was therefore referred to as the 1932 Pattern life-preserver. This was the main type used throughout the Battle of Britain. It was not equipped with any automatic inflation devices and instead aircrew had to inflate it by tube. These were known by another name, as Wing Commander Bob Foster once recalled: 'It was quite pleasant to sit out in the gardens in deck or other easy chairs while on readiness, our Mae Wests (buoyancy aids!) on.'[17] The nickname originated because someone wearing the inflated life-preserver often appeared to be as large-breasted as the American actress and singer Mary Jane 'Mae' West.

Aircrew were encouraged to fly with their 'Mae West' partially inflated, as well as a number of additional Kapok pads fitted, so that they had some initial buoyancy once in water. The issue colour was either a dark beige khaki or grey/green cotton, which, as mentioned, did little to assist with location in the murky waters of the Channel.

The 'Mae West' was basically a double thickness cotton waistcoat with three buttons at the front and webbing tapes which passed around the body and tied at the chest and waist. Later, in the Battle of Britain, some pilots were issued a pack of fluorescence, a greenish yellow dye in powdered form, to sew to their life jacket so that a pilot floating in the sea would leave a vivid stain on the surface of the water, though it is not clear if this was then standard issue or still an experimental item.

Many pilots and aircrew had their life-preservers spray-painted with chrome yellow aircraft paint in an effort to improve their visibility. This was recalled by Flight Lieutenant Jimmy Corbin DFC, who had to paint his life jacket the day he arrived on his first squadron during the Battle of Britain:

'We left the dispersal hut and collected our own inflatable life jackets. These were primitive affairs worn over the chest. They were covered in stout canvas and blown up by mouth and we spent the rest of the day painting them with yellow dope to make us more conspicuous should we bale out and end up the sea. Unbeknown to us the yellow dope made them highly flammable.'[18]

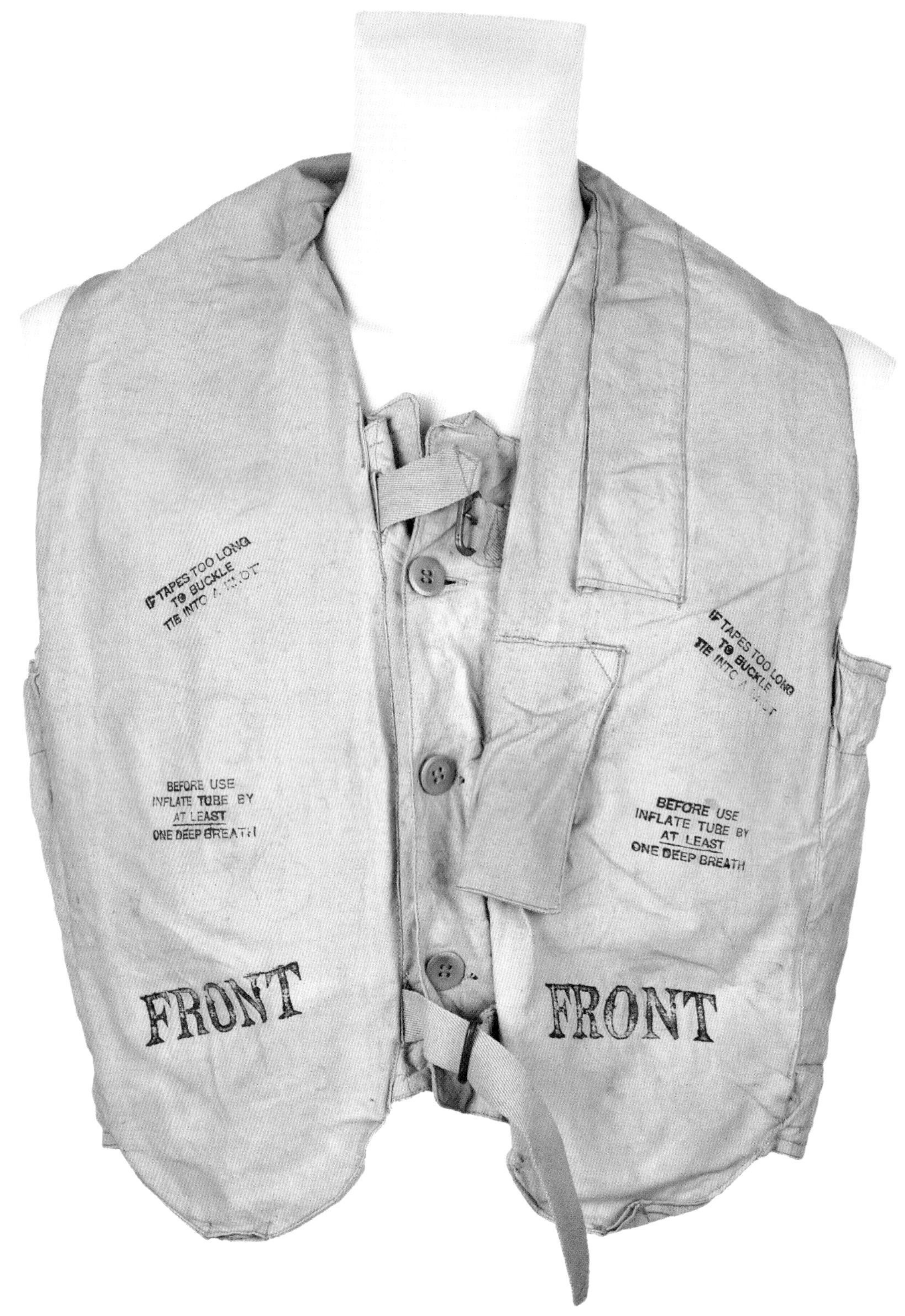
IF TAPES TOO LONG
TO BUCKLE
IF TAPES TOO LONG
TO BUCKLE
BEFORE USE
INFLATE TUBE BY
AT LEAST
ONE DEEP BREATH
FRONT
FRONT

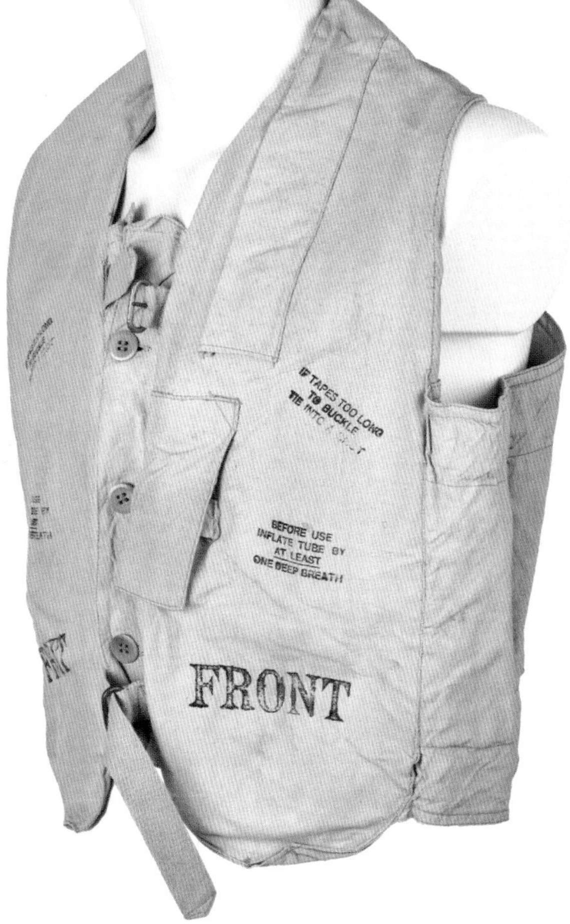

ABOVE, RIGHT and OPPOSITE: Three views of the 1932 Pattern life-preserver. It was inflated by mouth, although the inflation tube is missing on this particular example. A degree of buoyancy could be provided by inserted Kapok pads. Note the beige colour as supplied, leading to some aircrew spraying or painting them yellow to aid visibility. (Phil Phillips Collection)

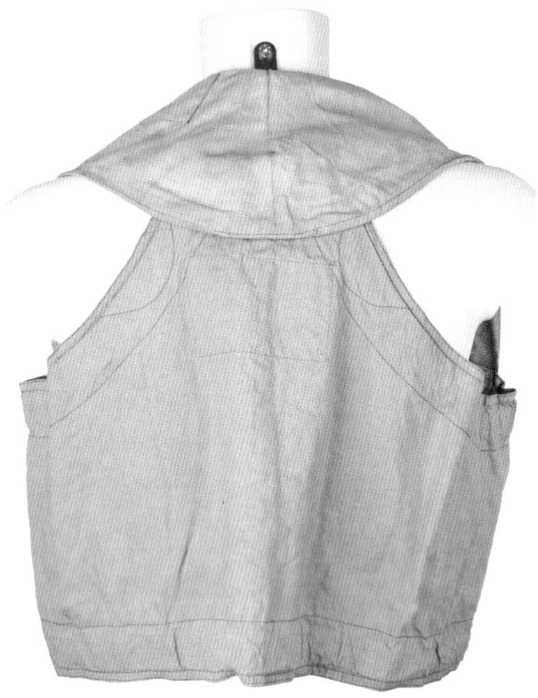

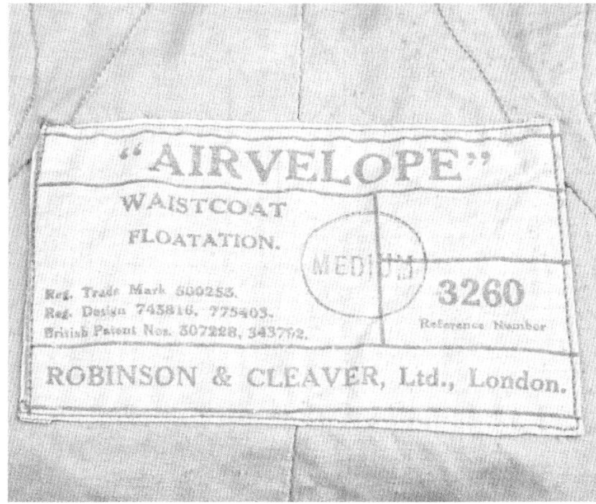

ABOVE: Manufacturer's label on a 1932 Pattern life-preserver. (Phil Phillips Collection)

LEFT: Rear view of the 1932 Pattern life-preserver. (Phil Phillips Collection)

ABOVE: A group of 602 (City of Glasgow) Squadron pilots, all from 'B' Flight, pictured outside one of the dispersal huts at RAF Westhampnett in the Battle of Britain. The only individuals who have been identified are Sergeant Douglas Elcome, far left, Flying Officer John Hart, third from right, and Flight Lieutenant Donald MacFarlane Jack, second from right. During close examination of this image it is possible to see the cracking off the paint applied to the life-preserver of the pilot standing to Hart's right. (The 602 (City of Glasgow) Squadron Museum)

An example of the 1932 Pattern life-preserver produced in a slightly different colour. Note that this one has the mouth top up tube. (Mick Prodger Collection)

A typical Battle of Britain period fighter pilot, Pilot Officer Osgood Villiers 'Pedro' Hanbury, poses in front of his fighter – in this a Spitfire of 602 (City of Glasgow) Squadron. Hanbury is wearing an unpainted 1932 Pattern life-preserver. Having joined the squadron on 3 September 1940, Hanbury soon made his mark, claiming two Dornier Do 17s on 7 and 12 September respectively, and a Bf 110 destroyed on 15 September. A shared Ju 88 was recorded on the 30th, a damaged Ju 88 on 5 October and finally a Bf 109 destroyed on 30 October. Hanbury did not survive the war, the aircraft he was travelling to Gibraltar in being shot down over the Bay of Biscay in 1943. (Andy Saunders Collection)

WAISTCOAT, LIFE SAVING, STOLE PATTERN, TROPICAL
Stores Reference: 22C/79

This version of the life-preserver is very similar to the temperate issue variety. The main difference between the two designs is that there is less material on the rear section of the Tropical variant, it lacking a full back. At the same time, there are no buttons to the front of the Tropical design, it only being secured by tapes. Instructions are again printed on the front of the waistcoat, and it also had to be inflated orally. It was the latter that led to some RAF pilots opted to use captured Luftwaffe life-preservers if available.

It seems that Group Captain Charles Kingcome DSO, DFC & Bar was one of those who felt that the Luftwaffe 'Mae Wests' were a better option that the issued RAF kit: 'The German life-jacket was in many ways superior to our British issue, being, among other things, inflated by a small compressed air bottle rather than by lung power. It was also less bulky and far more comfortable. It seemed unlikely that the late demigod would find much use for it in Valhalla, so I relieved him of it and wore it continually until I was posted abroad two years later.

>>>

Tropical version of the RAF's 1932 Pattern life-preserver, which, though not the main issue type, was used by aircrew during the Battle of Britain. (Mick Prodger Collection)

Pilots of 32 Squadron's 'B' Flight resting between sorties at RAF Hawkinge, 29 July 1940. A number of them are wearing 1932 Pattern life-preservers. Although this is almost certainly a staged image, in reality many pilots preferred to fly wearing their service shoes, as seen here, rather than flying boots. (ww2images)

An RAF fighter pilot pictured soon after his life-preserver had done what it was intended to do. This image depicts the rescue of 602 (City of Glasgow) Squadron's Sergeant Pilot Cyril Babbage at Bognor Regis on 26 August 1940. Babbage had engaged a Bf 109, shooting it down, only to then be attacked by *Hauptmann* Mayer of 1/*JG* 53. His Spitfire, X4118, was severely damaged and he took to his parachute. Babbage was awarded a Distinguished Flying Medal on 25 October 1940. (Andy Saunders Collection)

'On reflection, I was probably lucky never to have been shot down over water at that time. With no routine inspection of the air bottle or the airtight jacket – which unlike ours, had no built-in buoyancy – I suspect the garment might well have gradually lost its effectiveness and dragged me bubbling to the bottom.'[19]

IRVIN HARNESS SUIT
Stores Reference: 15A/276-278, 15A/294 AND 305

The idea of the harness suit was to save space for gunners in the confined environments of their turrets. Rather than having to carry extra equipment, the idea was that the parachute would be combined with the flying suit. Such designs were mainly used by air gunners in the Boulton Paul Defiant, as well as some Blenheim crew members.

With the concept hailing back to the 1930s, the Irvin Air Chute was manufactured from a heavy olive drab cotton material. Without arms or legs, it contained a full parachute harness and cartridge inflating life-preserver bladder. Although a sound concept, the Irvin suit was not very popular with aircrew.

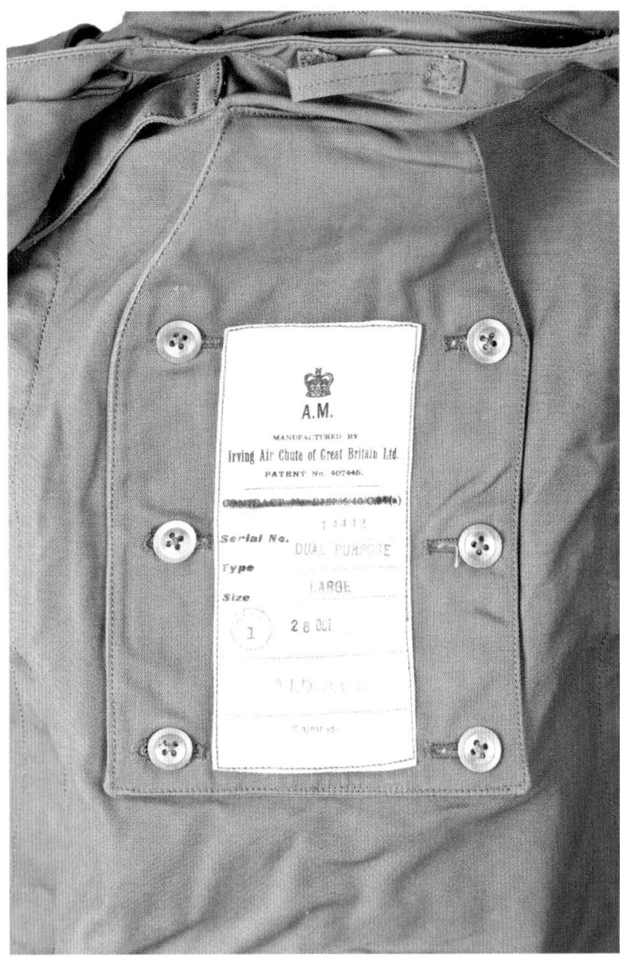

RIGHT and OPPOSITE: An example of the Irvin Harness Suit (Stores Reference 15A/276-278 and 15A/294 and 305) utilised by Blenheim and Defiant crews. (Phil Phillips Collection)

GQ PARASUIT

The Gerald Quilter Parachute Company was awarded a contract by the Air Ministry in 1940 to develop a suit especially for the rear gunner of the Boulton Paul Defiant.

One air gunner who remembers that the Air Ministry was worried about the Defiant's cramped rear turret was Sergeant Albert Gregory of 141 Squadron: 'The turret on the Defiant was a mid-upper with four guns. I personally found no problem getting into and out of the turret but an Air Ministry declaration came to all squadrons on Defiants saying that any air gunner above 5 foot 10" would be considered too tall for the turret and they were to be posted.'[20]

The Defiant was initially used in the Battle of Britain in a daylight role, but with no forward-facing armament, the Luftwaffe fighter pilots soon got its measure and it was relegated to night fighter duties. Unfortunately, the rear turret was so small a conventional parachute or even a harness suit would not enable a gunner to get out of the escape hatch in an emergency and therefore a suit was required that contained everything including the harness, parachute with the shroud lines within the quilted back panels and an orally inflated stole for buoyancy. It was this concept that led to the GQ Parasuit.

LEFT and OPPOSITE: A series of photographs showing the construction of the now very rare GQ Parasuit which was designed specifically for the Boulton Paul Defiant rear gunner and use in the very cramped turret. (Phil Phillips Collection)

Two members of aircrew from 141 Squadron pictured in front of a Boulton Paul Defiant. The individual on the right is Pilot Officer John Rushton Gard'ner, a New Zealander. The air-gunner to his right is wearing the GQ Parasuit, supplied exclusively to Defiant gunners, which incorporates a parachute harness and life-preserver. (London Battle of Britain Monument Website)

PARACHUTE, SINGLE POINT, QUICK RELEASE WITH SEAT PACK, TYPE C-2
Stores References: 15A/197, Pack Only 15A/96

This was the most common type of parachute worn by RAF fighter pilots in the Battle of Britain. It differed from the earlier Type C in that it had a large D-ring on a wide canvas belt around the waist which was much easier to locate when tumbling through the air after baling out.

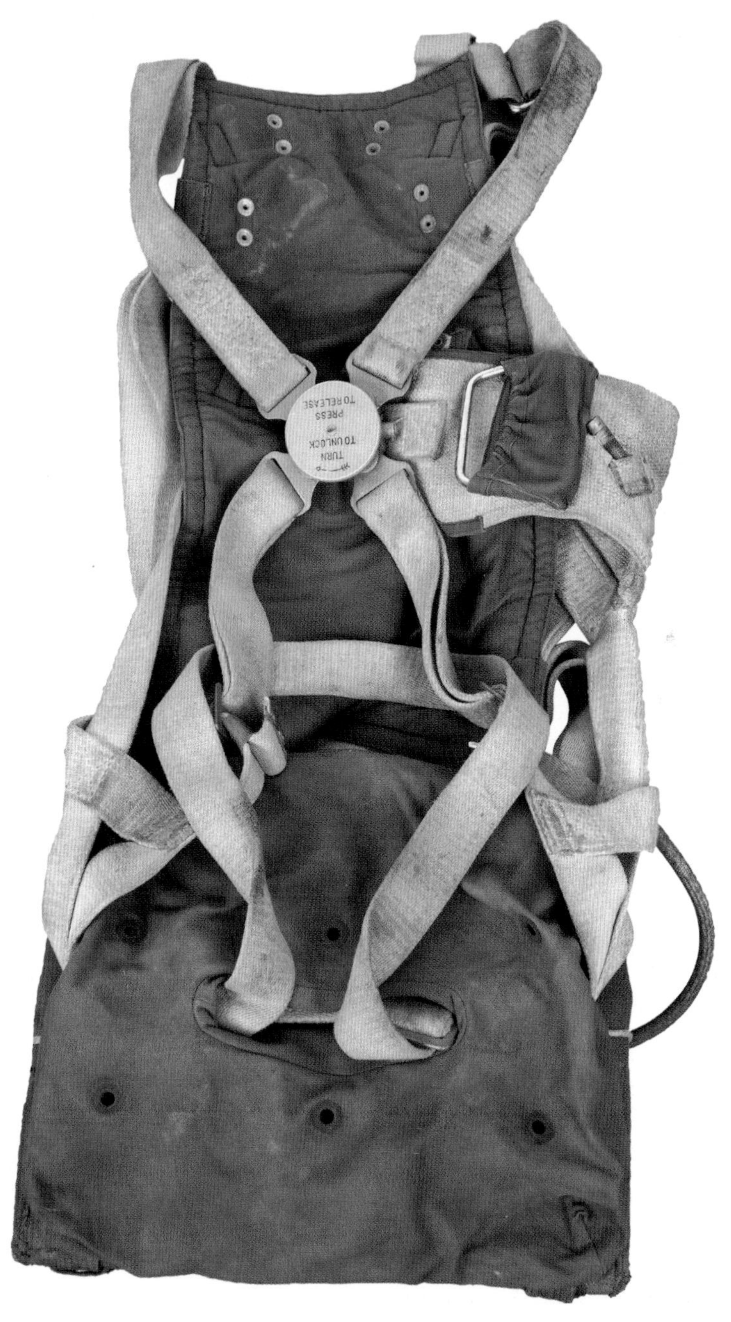

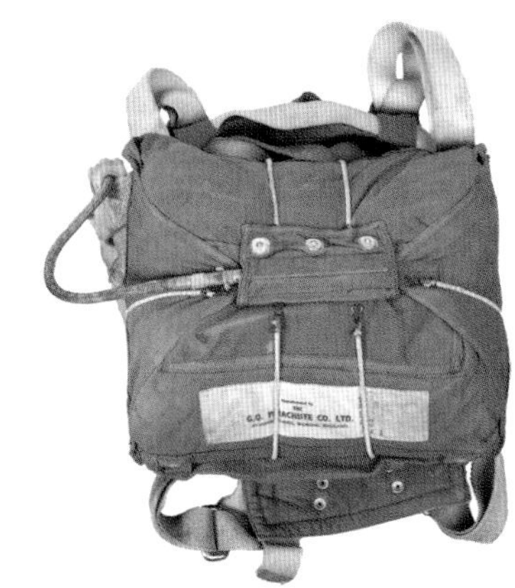

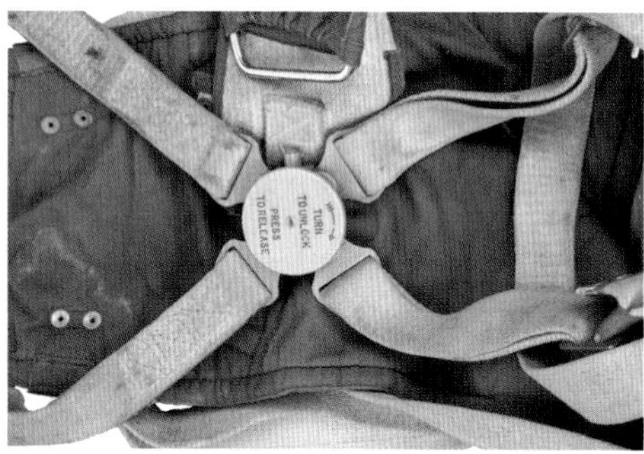

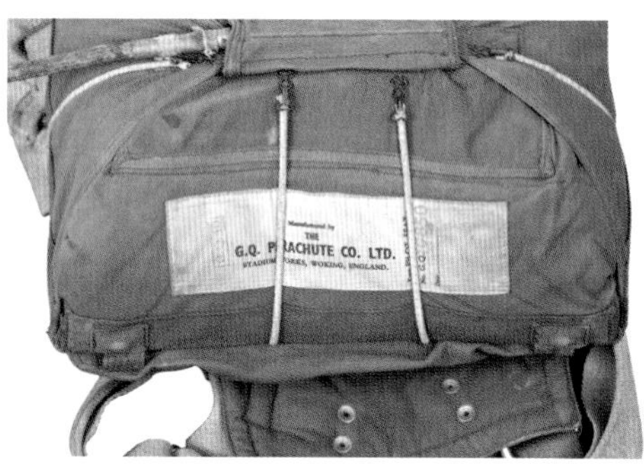

ABOVE and PREVIOUS PAGE: A series of photographs of the Parachute, Single Point, Quick Release with seat pack, Type C-2, which was the most common type used by Fighter Command pilots in 1940. This particular example was manufactured by GQ and is dated January 1940. (Phil Phillips Collection)

All of the parachutes worn had a common feature of a quick release box in to which all the webbings straps locate. On hitting the ground in strong winds, or if about to land on water, it was essential for a pilot or member of aircrew to be able to release himself quickly to either prevent being dragged across fields or drown if water filled up the canopy or being tangled up in the rigging lines. The parachute pack itself formed the seat cushion which located into the aircraft's seat.

Aircraftsman Joe Roddis, a fitter with 234 Squadron at Middle Wallop in the Battle of Britain, remembered that his pilot used to like his parachute left in the cockpit at readiness: 'I recall that Bob Doe used to have his parachute in the cockpit, as the pilots ran to the aircraft we would be in the cockpit and start the aircraft for them and jump out to help them strap in, other pilots use to like to have their chutes left on the wing of the aircraft.'

One pilot who was unfortunate enough to be hit in the fuel tank of his Hurricane by return fire from a Dornier Do 215, and therefore had to resort to his parachute, was Wing Commander Geoffrey Page DSO, DFC. Despite an intense fire in his cockpit, which left him terribly burned, Page managed to bale out: 'I tumbled. Sky, sea, sky, over and over as a clearing brain issued instructions to out flung limbs: "Pull the ripcord-right hand to the ripcord".'[21]

Despite a delay due to the considerable pain from his hands, Page managed to deploy the canopy: 'With a jerk the silken canopy billowed out in the clear summer sky.'

A group of aircrew pictured wearing a variety of flying clothing and equipment. The individuals seen fourth and fifth from the left in the front row are both wearing the harness for the Parachute, Single-point, Quick Release. The left-hand of the two is carrying the Chest Pack under his left arm, whilst the second man has the Pack hanging from the harness on his front. (Mark Hillier Collection)

PARACHUTE, SINGLE-POINT, QUICK RELEASE WITH TWO-POINT DETACHABLE CHEST PACK (OBSERVER TYPE)

Stores References: Harness 15A/137, Pack 15A/141

This parachute was used mainly by aircrew serving in larger aircraft as it was less bulky than the seat type and could allow more freedom of movement around the crew positions. This style of parachute would have been used by some of the Blenheim crews during the Battle of Britain.

The webbing straps have a similar appearance to the seat type parachute, also being fitted with a quick release box. There are two large safety hooks on the chest straps to take the steel loops fitted to the parachute pack. The rip cord was fitted on the pack.

An example of the Parachute, Single-point, Quick Release, with the two-point detachable Chest Pack (Observer Type), which, with the stores reference 15A/137 for the harness and 15A/141 for the pack, was used mainly by Observers and crew in the Blenheim. (Simon Lannoy Collection)

Section 8
SERVICE DRESS AND NON-FLYING EQUIPMENT

As mentioned previously, officers were expected to source their own service uniform, as explained by paragraph 185 of the 1940-dated edition of *The King's Regulations*: 'An officer, on first appointment to a commission, will be required to provide himself with the compulsory articles of kit laid down in AP 1358, Appendix I. He will be required to maintain his kit in good order and to the scale laid down, at his own expense, and to equip himself with any additional articles ordered to be worn.' An initial kit allowance was given to officers to provide themselves with the basics.

Airmen and NCOs were, however, entitled to all of their kit at the public expense. The scale of provision of this kit was laid down in AP 830. A further entry in AP 958 (paragraph 2526) details that each airman, 'on final acceptance for regular air force service will receive a free issue of personal clothing and necessaries, and accoutrements'. However, some items were not included. This included 'razors, tooth-brushes and hair combs are not supplied as part of the initial outfit, but an allowance of one shilling and sixpence towards the cost of these items will be credited to the account of each recruit'.

SERVICE DRESS TUNIC AND TROUSERS, OFFICERS

The reality was that the majority of the pilots chose to fly in their service uniform or No.5 Service, Home dress rather than wear a bulky flying suit. In part this may have been due to the hot weather in much of the summer of 1940, some aircrew often opted to fly in just shirtsleeves.

The RAF officers' jacket at this stage of the war was of the 1919 style, this being readily identified by both the large, external, 'bellows' pockets on the skirt of the tunic and by four brass-button fastenings, features that were carried over from the earlier Army uniforms of the RFC. The jacket is belted at the waist with a brass buckle and the jacket has the belt sewn to it at the rear.

The jacket was usually made of barathea wool and in a shade of blue-grey, although there could be differences in colour between tailors. Personal preferences may have dictated variations in styling and cut, as described by Wing Commander Patrick 'Paddy' Barthropp DFC, AFC: 'At this time West End tailors attended the Officers' Mess to kit us out with our various uniforms which included Mess kit with very tight-fitting trousers. The cutters would always pose the question "Which side do you dress on, sir?"'[22]

Air Commodore John Ellacombe CB, DFC & Bar also commented that the 'uniform allowance in those days was forty pounds, and that was enough to buy you two uniforms, lots of shirts, several shoes and everything else. I think Burberrys was a very expensive place. You paid four pounds for a uniform. If you went to Alkits, you got one for about two pounds fifty.'[23]

Using their allowance, officers would have purchased all of their kit, including the brown leather gloves to wear with their service dress, which some pilots personalised, as Squadron Leader Nigel Rose AE once recalled: 'Being an RAF fighter pilot (top button of your tunic undone) gave one a definite feel of pride and perhaps importance.'[24]

Some of the Auxiliary Air Force squadrons went one step further. The men of 601 (County of London) Squadron, for example, had unique uniforms tailored with linings of bright red silk.

The officers rank braid was sewn to the cuffs of each sleeve and flying brevets were worn central over the left-hand breast pocket.

Officers from the Royal Australian Air Force had a different colour uniform material. This was noted by Geoffrey Quill, who was attached to 64 Squadron during the Battle of Britain: 'I was also glad to meet the Flight Commander of "A" Flight, Gordon Olive, wearing the dark blue uniform of the RAAF.'[25]

An officer's service dress with belted waist, flight lieutenant rank braid on the sleeves and the four brass buttons. Note the padded King's Crown wings. (Phil Phillips Collection)

ABOVE: An example of a Warrant Officer pilot's service dress showing the rank badges (commonly referred to as the 'Tate and Lyles' – a reference to the similarity to the logo used by the Tate and Lyle Company) on the sleeves and padded King's Crown pilots' wings. (Simon Lannoy Collection)

BELOW: Pilots of 19 Squadron resting at RAF Fowlmere in September 1940. Note the Fleet Air Arm pilot wearing his navy-blue service dress with 1936 Pattern boots and a 'Mae West'. The RAF officer on the left is wearing his service tunic, whilst the individual on the right appears to be sporting a 'Prestige' flying suit.

Flying Officer John Reginald Hardacre, of 504 Squadron, pictured before his death on 30 September 1940 – this being the date he was shot down over the South West in Hurricane P3414. Hardacre is seen here wearing what appears to be a privately tailored RAF version of the Army's battledress. The RAF was later to adopt an official version of the battledress, its version being known as Suits, Aircrew, later called the War Service Dress. (Battle of Britain Memorial Trust)

The majority of other nationalities who flew during the Battle of Britain wore RAF uniforms that were then differentiated by shoulder flashes indicating the officer's country of origin. One exception to this was the Armée de l'Air uniform, which was designed after the French regulation 1928 air service uniform. It was dark blue with a single row of four gold buttons and a golden stripe on each shoulder. The rank insignia was on the sleeves, just like the Army and Navy at that time.

Fleet Air Arm pilots seconded to RAF squadrons during the Battle also wore their standard dark blue Royal Navy officers' uniforms. These had two rows of gold Royal Navy button down the front. The jacket was un-belted and the wings were on the left sleeve above the rank braid and not above the breast pocket. They mainly used standard issue RAF flying equipment.

Service dress trousers were originally of a high-waisted pattern with swallow-tailed back and peaked front, as was the general fashion of the day to accommodate braces, though by the 1940s fashion had dictated a move towards a more modern waist fitting.

SERVICE DRESS TUNIC AND TROUSERS, OTHER RANKS

The sergeant pilots' uniform was made under contract for the Air Ministry. Though they were much heavier and of poorer quality serge, they were similar in cut to the officers' uniform, again belted but differing from the officers in that the belt was detachable. Rank badges worn on the sleeves. The uniforms were tailored with a 'Faux cuff' or stitched pleat on the arms.

ABOVE and RIGHT: The Airmans' service dress seen here has a similar style to the Officers', though the difference in material can clearly be seen with a much heavier serge was used. Again, the uniform is belted, the rank badges for NCOs being worn on the sleeve halfway between the elbow and the shoulder. This particular example belonged to a corporal of the Auxiliary Air Force; note the Auxiliary shoulder title insignia under the eagle. (Phil Phillips Collection)

A Sergeant pilot's uniform and forage cap, again showing the coarseness of the material used. Note the cloth eagle insignia on the arm, which is specific to NCOs. (Simon Lannoy Collection)

Seen here on the far right, Battle of Britain pilot Sergeant Roy Norman Cooper is wearing his service dress uniform and 1939 Pattern boots. The pilot to Cooper's right is wearing the iconic Irvin jacket and B Type helmet with Mk.IIIa goggles. Roy Norman Cooper, of Portsmouth, joined the RAFVR in July 1939 as an Airman u/t Pilot. Called up on 1 September, Cooper completed his flying training and joined 610 Squadron at Acklington on 6 October 1940. Cooper was killed on 28 October 1945. (Mark Hillier Collection)

SHIRT AND TIE

Officers used to wear a light blue shirt made from 'end on end' material, often by Van Heusen. These had detachable collars which were not very popular with aircrew as they had the ability to shrink and strangle the wearer when saturated. Other NCO personnel wore duller blue-grey coloured shirts.

Wing Commander Geoffrey Page DSO, DFC, was definitely of the opinion that the shirts and ties were not suitable apparel for air combat in the Battle: 'Midway across the Channel I was learning a painful lesson. To my discomfort I was discovering that you cannot wear a collar and tie and fly on operational sorties. The continuous twisting of the head to search the skies called for something less cutting than the sharp edge of a semi-starched collar.' With one hand 'endeavouring to grope beneath the many encumbrances and so remove the offending article', Page managed to slide back the hood and throw the collar out into the sea.

Squadron Leader Geoffrey Wellum DFC had similar recollections: 'I remove my tie and open the collar of my shirt (far less sore on the back of my neck when you keep looking round). Now, where's my silk scarf? Don't say it's been lost. I take my parachute from the locker and, of course, my scarf is where I last threw it. I tie it round my neck, pick up my helmet and slinging the chute over my shoulder, and head for the door.'[26]

The officers' and NCOs' ties were all a plain black pattern.

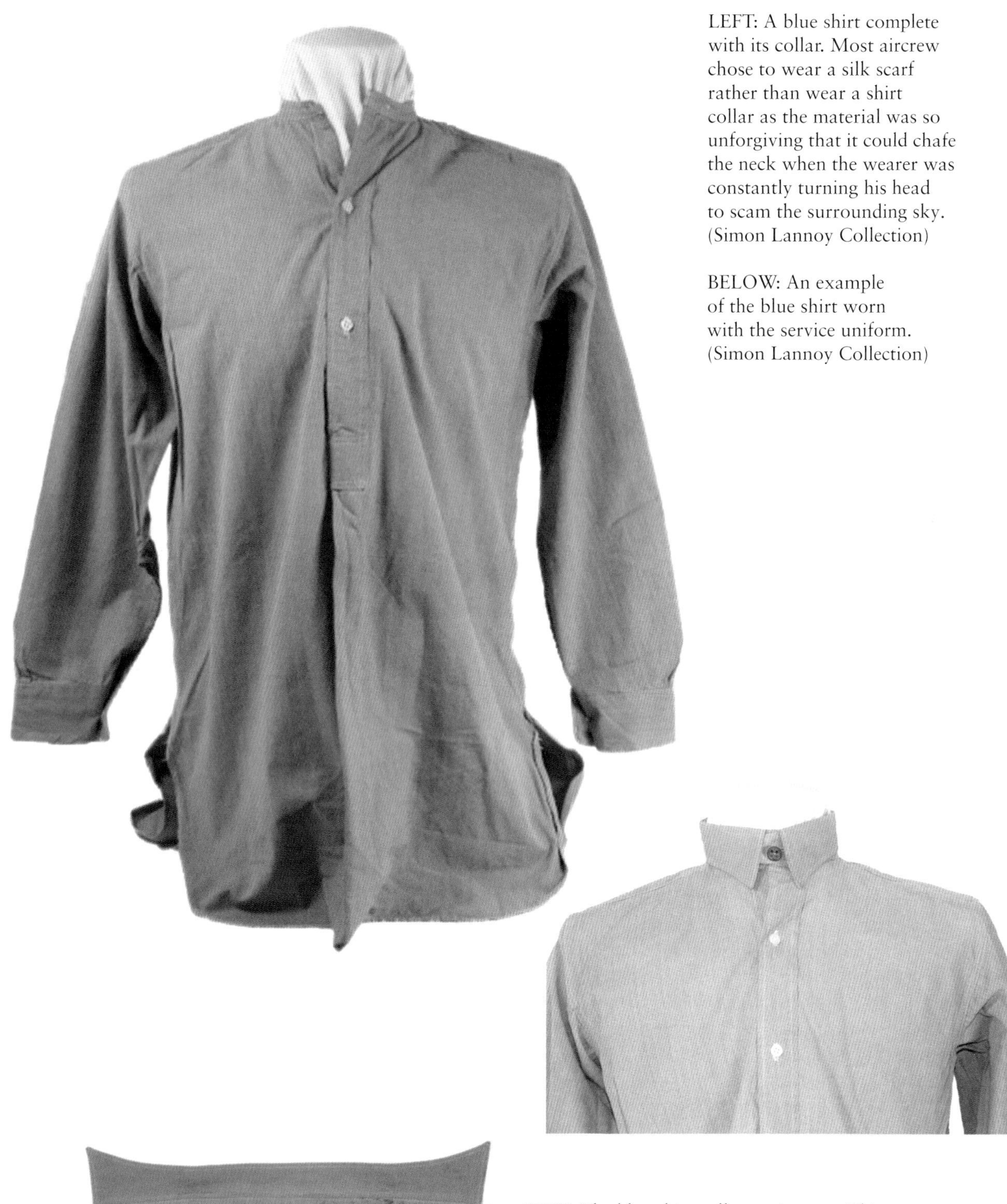

LEFT: A blue shirt complete with its collar. Most aircrew chose to wear a silk scarf rather than wear a shirt collar as the material was so unforgiving that it could chafe the neck when the wearer was constantly turning his head to scam the surrounding sky. (Simon Lannoy Collection)

BELOW: An example of the blue shirt worn with the service uniform. (Simon Lannoy Collection)

LEFT: The blue shirt collar on its own. This example is 1947 dated. (Simon Lannoy Collection)

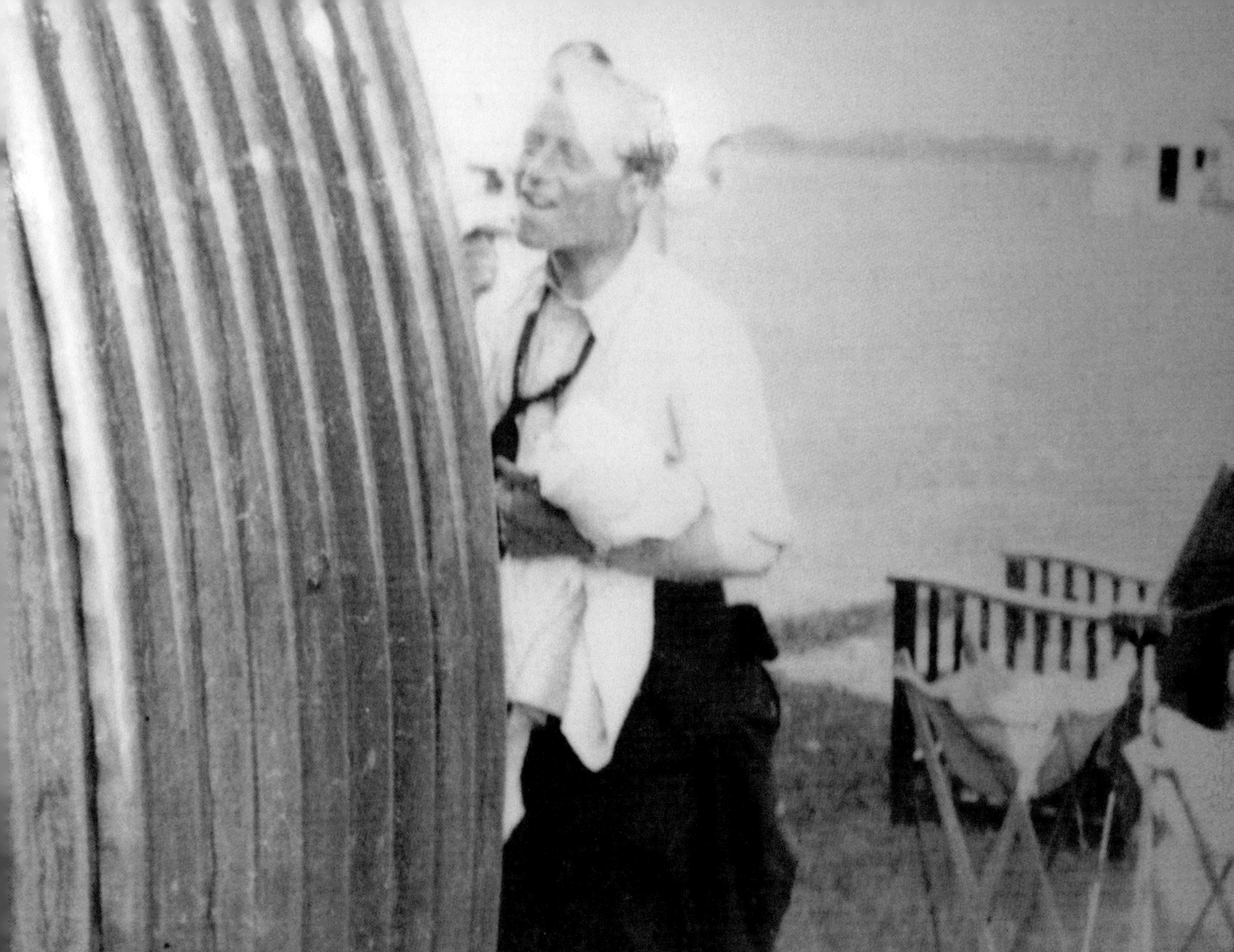

Pictured in shirt and tie, 145 Squadron's Flight Lieutenant Adrian Hope Boyd manages to have a shave whilst at readiness outside the 'B' Flight hut at RAF Westhampnett during the Battle of Britain. (Tangmere Military Aviation Museum)

AIRCREW TIME PIECES AND STOP WATCH
Stores References: 6B/159 (Time Piece), 6B/117 (Stopwatch)

Since the early 1930s the need for an accurate time piece for aircrew was recognised by the Air Ministry. In 1939, it was realised that there would be a need for a greater quantity of watches and through Goldsmiths and Silversmiths Co. Ltd approaches were made to various Swiss watchmakers, including manufacturers such as Longines, Omega, Movado and Jaeger Le Coultre. These time pieces were all designated the Mk.VIIa and given the Stores Reference 6B/159. The watches are marked as such on the rear of the case. They can normally be dated by a serial number or date within the rear cover. It is thought that the watches were actually issued to observers and not to the fighter pilots.

The Fleet Air Arm pilots had their own watch which was procured through the RN Hydropgraphic Service and identified as the HS8. Manufactured by the same Swiss sources as the RAF examples, they were identical in appearance – apart from the case being solid Nickel to avoid corrosion in salty atmospheres.

The Mk.III stopwatch was issued to observers and navigators of larger aircraft, such as the Blenheim, as an alternative. Once again, the stopwatch is marked on the rear with the stores reference and sometimes the date.

LEFT: The front of the very rare Movado watch, as issued to aircrew, this one dated 1940. (Simon Lannoy Collection)

BELOW: The rear of the Movado watch showing the Air Ministry mark. (Simon Lannoy Collection)

BELOW RIGHT: The rear of the Mk.III stopwatch showing its Stores Reference of 6B/117, date of 1940 and Air Ministry marks. (Mark Hillier Collection)

LEFT: The face of the Mk.III stopwatch as issued to Blenheim aircrew. (Mark Hillier Collection)

NON-FLYING HEADGEAR

Pilots and aircrew all required headdress to complete their uniforms. Many kept their forage caps with them whilst flying in case they had to put down at other RAF stations.

The NCO aircrew would be issued with a forage cap known as the Field Service Cap, this being made available for the first time in 1936. Officers also has the option to wear this cap, although

>>>

ABOVE: The officers' service dress hat. These were commonly made or supplied by a variety of tailors, but each to essentially the same pattern. The officers' cap badge is made from gold and silver wire. (Phil Phillips Collection)

RIGHT: The inside of an officer's service dress hat showing the tailor's details, the leather sweatband and the peak from the underside. (Phil Phillips Collection)

they also had the service dress hat. The NCO version was tailored from a coarse blue/grey serge material, the cap badge being an RAF monogram badge made of brass with a King's Crown. The officers' version was tailored from softer barathea wool with an RAF eagle badge with a King's Crown above it. This would be provided by each individual tailor as appointed by the officer concerned.

There is evidence that officers had a best No.1 hat with a flatter top and bigger peak for formal parades and functions, as well as a 'slouch' hat for operations. Officers had to purchase a service dress peaked cap, which was again constructed again from barathea wool with a stiffened peak. The cap has a black chin strap around the peak, with a King's Crown gold wire braid badge, with eagle in the centre, above.

The issue Warrant Officers' hat was of a similar pattern to the officers' version, but with a black shiny peak instead of a cloth peak. It also had its own style of badge.

ABOVE: NCO aircrew would wear the Field Service Cap and did not have a service dress hat. The material is quite course serge. The cap badge is brass with two lugs on the back secured through the material with a split pin. There are two small RAF brass buttons on the front of the cap. (Phil Phillips Collection)

BELOW: An example of the RAF officers' field service cap, the difference being the finer material and the cap badge being a brass eagle with King's Crown above. (Phil Phillips Collection)

ABOVE and RIGHT: A boxed Armée de l'Air officer's service dress hat. A number of Free French pilots flew during the Battle of Britain wearing their own uniforms and insignia. (Phil Phillips Collection)

A 1940-dated Polish Air Force officer's service dress hat, with the Polish Air Force badge in gold wire. During the Battle of Britain, some Polish, Australian and, as mentioned, Free French pilots wore the uniforms of their nations. Many also flew in RAF uniform with distinguishing country flashes worn on the shoulder of the service uniform. (Simon Lannoy Collection)

ABOVE: Two Polish pilots from 303 Squadron – Pilot Officer Jan Zumbach (on the left) and Pilot Officer Miroslaw Feric – pictured with the squadron's puppy mascot at RAF Leconfield on 24 October 1940. Both men are wearing a 1932 Pattern life-preserver. Zumbach is wearing a Polish officers' service cap, whilst Feric has a D Type oxygen mask and B Type flying helmet. (Piotr Sikora Collection)

LEFT: An example of the typical Royal Navy officers' hat as would have been worn by members of the Fleet Air Arm who were operational with Fighter Command in the Battle of Britain.
(Simon Lannoy Collection)

SERVICE SHOES

The shoes worn by both officers and NCOs were of the Oxford Pattern or style, with a toe cap in black leather. The officers' shoes were again purchased through their tailors.

SOCKS

Issue socks were available. Known as 'sea boot socks', they came in cream or light grey heavy wool, though pilots frequently wore their own private purchase examples.

BRACES

The standard braces issued to all British servicemen during the Second World War were off-white in colour. They were made entirely from cotton with leather button attachments. Most were stamped with Air Ministry marks. The officers' braces were usually supplied by their tailor.

The Oxford Pattern shoe of the style worn by both officers and airmen. Many pilots chose to wear shoes whilst flying, despite the fact that they gave little protection to the ankle and often led to severe burns in the case of a fire. (Phil Phillips Collection)

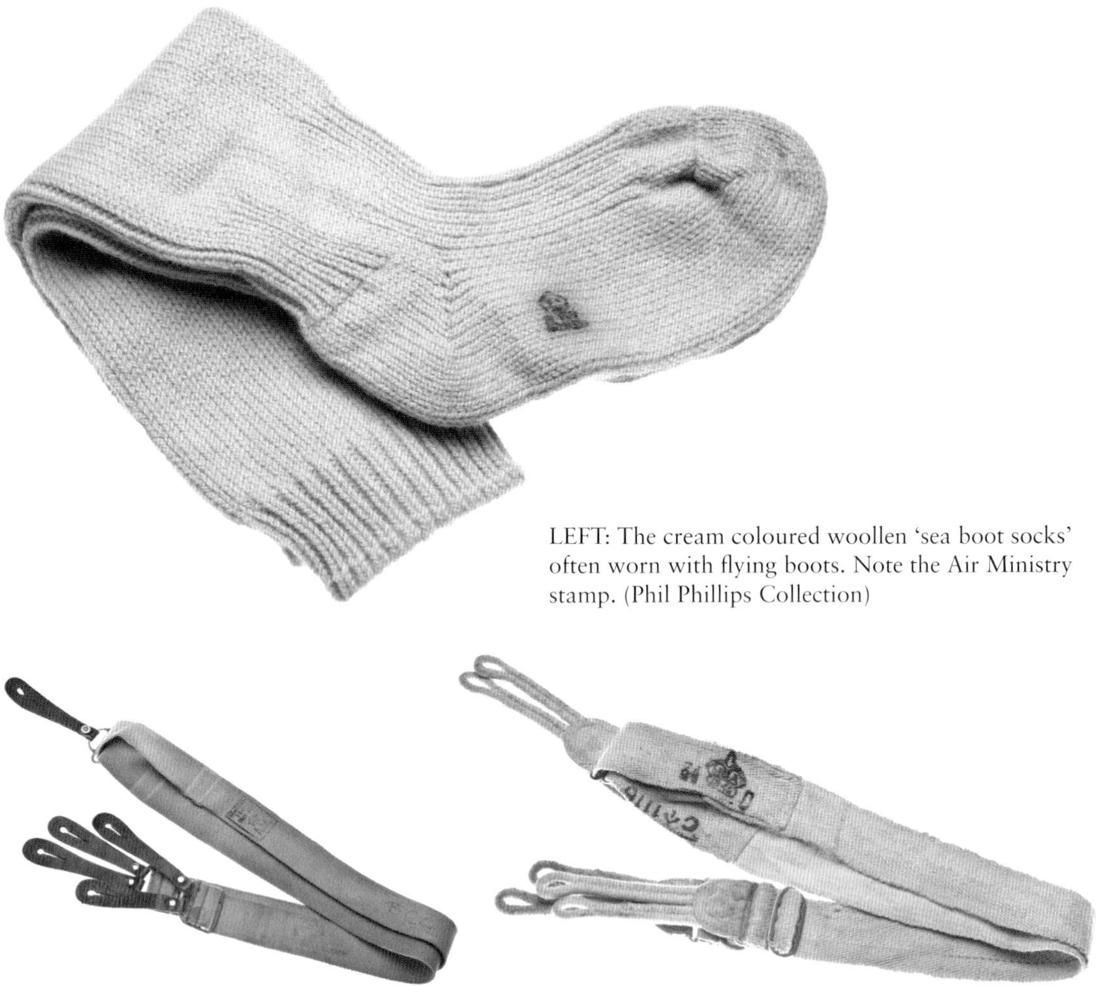

LEFT: The cream coloured woollen 'sea boot socks' often worn with flying boots. Note the Air Ministry stamp. (Phil Phillips Collection)

ABOVE: Two views of RAF issue braces. The Air Ministry markings can clearly be seen and both sets are dated 1940. (Phil Phillips Collection)

STEEL HELMET AND GAS MASK

There are few photographs of on duty aircrew carrying either a steel helmet or a gas mask during the Battle of Britain period. During the early war years, it was compulsory for RAF ground personnel, including officers, to carry their respirator (gas mask) and steel helmet with them at all times whilst on duty. The steel helmet, commonly known as a 'Battle Bowler', would have been in the standard RAF blue/grey colour scheme.

The steel helmet available in the Battle was either the Mk.Ia Brodie helmet or the Mk.II, which was fitted with an elasticated (actually, sprung) webbing chin strap. These helmets were frequently seen being carried on the outside of a respirator haversack, held in place by the helmet's chinstrap.

Although the Mk.IVa respirator was still available and in use, the standard respirator for that time was the Mk.V, which was introduced in 1939. It was carried in a beige Mk.VII haversack.

ABOVE and RIGHT: A Mk.II steel helmet, this example being dated 1939. The RAF issue helmets were commmonly blue/grey in colour, although some were green as shown here. (Simon Lannoy Collection)

LEFT: A Mk.IV respirator. Despite the fact that the Mk.V became available in 1939, the Mk.IV was still being used by the RAF in 1940. (Phil Phillips Collection)

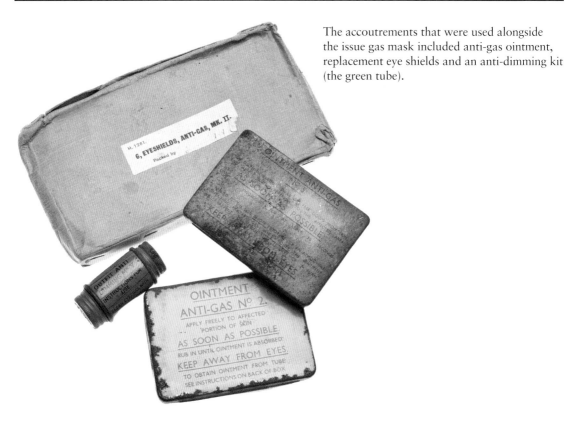

The accoutrements that were used alongside the issue gas mask included anti-gas ointment, replacement eye shields and an anti-dimming kit (the green tube).

GREATCOATS

Both officers and NCOs were issued with greatcoats. The NCOs variant was made of heavy blue/grey serge with two rows of King's Crown buttons down the front, four buttons in each.

Made of a lighter, higher quality material, the officers' greatcoat differed in that it was constructed from a fleece cloth and had two rows of five brass buttons. It was also belted.

NCO ranks would be found on the sleeve with the RAF eagle on the shoulder. Ranks were displayed on shoulder boards on officers' greatcoats. Officers' greatcoats again would have been supplied by the tailor.

IDENTITY DISCS

RAF service personnel were issued with two pressed fibre identity discs made of vulcanised asbestos fibre. The two-disc system was introduced into the British armed forces in September 1916. One of the discs was green in colour, and octagonal in shape; the second was a red round disc.

Paragraph 2104 of *The King's Regulations* stated: 'The identity discs prepared for an airman on attestation, in accordance with para 2104, will consist of one No.1 (green) disc, which will be suspended from the cord wound round the neck, and one No.2 (red) disc will be suspended from the No.1 (green) disc.'

The identity discs were hand-stamped with the surname, initials, service number and religion of the holder. For the serving in the Royal Air Force, the initials 'RAF' were also added.

ABOVE: Personnel of 234 Squadron at St Eval at the end of September 1940. The squadron had been posted to St Eval for a period of rest and to re-equip after a hectic time at RAF Middle Wallop. Note the officers in the front row wearing greatcoats, and the one pilot on the far left on operational readiness with his flying kit and 39 Pattern boots on. (Mark Hillier Collection)

RIGHT: Three sergeant aircrew of 235 Squadron, which operated Blenheims during the Battle of Britain. This photograph was taken late in 1940; note all three are wearing an NCO greatcoat, gas mask bag and 1936 Pattern flying boots. (Mark Hillier Collection)

An airman's issue greatcoat showing the very coarse material and four brass King's Crown buttons in two rows, not belted. (Phil Phillips Collection)

A greatcoat worn by a Leading Aircraftsman, though the sergeant rank badges of NCO aircrew would have been in a similar position on the sleeve. Note the RAF eagle badge on the shoulder; these were provided in pairs and are left and right handed. (Phil Phillips Collection)

ABOVE: The compressed fibre identity discs which were issued to Pilot Officer Harold Arthur Cooper Bird-Wilson. Bird-Wilson joined the RAF in 1937, going on to fly Hurricanes in the Battle of France and the Battle of Britain with 17 Squadron. He was shot down by Adolf Galland on 24 September 1940. Having baled out, he was rescued, badly burned, from the Channel by an MTB. He served throughout the war and became a squadron commander and wing leader. He eventually retired from the RAF as Air Vice-Marshal H. Bird-Wilson CBE, DSO, DFC & Bar, AFC & Bar. (Mark Hillier Collection)

OPPOSITE: RAF officers' greatcoat which was belted and of a fleece material. These were normally privately tailored. (Simon Lannoy Collection)

KIT BAG

NCO aircrew were issued with a white canvas duffle bag on which they would stencil their name and service number. Officers generally had suitcases or trunks, although they too could obtain a kit bag if desired or required.

A typical RAF kit bag issued to NCO aircrew. Dated 1940 and manufactured from a canvas type material, these items often had a name or service number stencilled on the front. Officers would have had private luggage. (Simon Lannoy Collection)

LOG BOOK

The flying log book issued to all aircrew during the Battle of Britain was an official document. Pilots' log books were known as Form 414, of which *The King's Regulations* stated: 'Every officer of the general duties branch of and below the rank of group captain and every airman pilot will keep a complete record in Form 414 of all flights undertaken by him, the log book being maintained in accordance with the instructions in the form.'

Each log book was used to record a pilot's qualifications, as well as maintain a log of his solo and dual flying and time as a passenger. The pilot was also required to present his log book for inspection on a monthly basis so that it could be certified as correct by the CO or his representative. This process was also undertaken annually.

It was not unusual during the Battle of Britain for pilots to also summarise the duty that they were engaged with. Some entries might also contain brief accounts of combats and victories, or losses of comrades.

An observers' and air gunners' log book of the type issued during the early part of the Second World War. These carried the identification reference Form 1767, whilst the pilots' log book was Form 414. This log book was issued to Sergeant Charles West, an observer of 59 Squadron which operated Blenheim Mk.IVs from RAF Thorney Island during the Battle of Britain period. West returned to operations in August 1940 after receiving wounds from a marauding Bf 109 which had chased his aircraft back across the Channel in early July, resulting in a crash landing. Although this squadron did carry out patrols on behalf of Fighter Command, it was not entitled to wear the Battle of Britain Clasp on the 1939-1945 Star. (Simon Lannoy Collection)

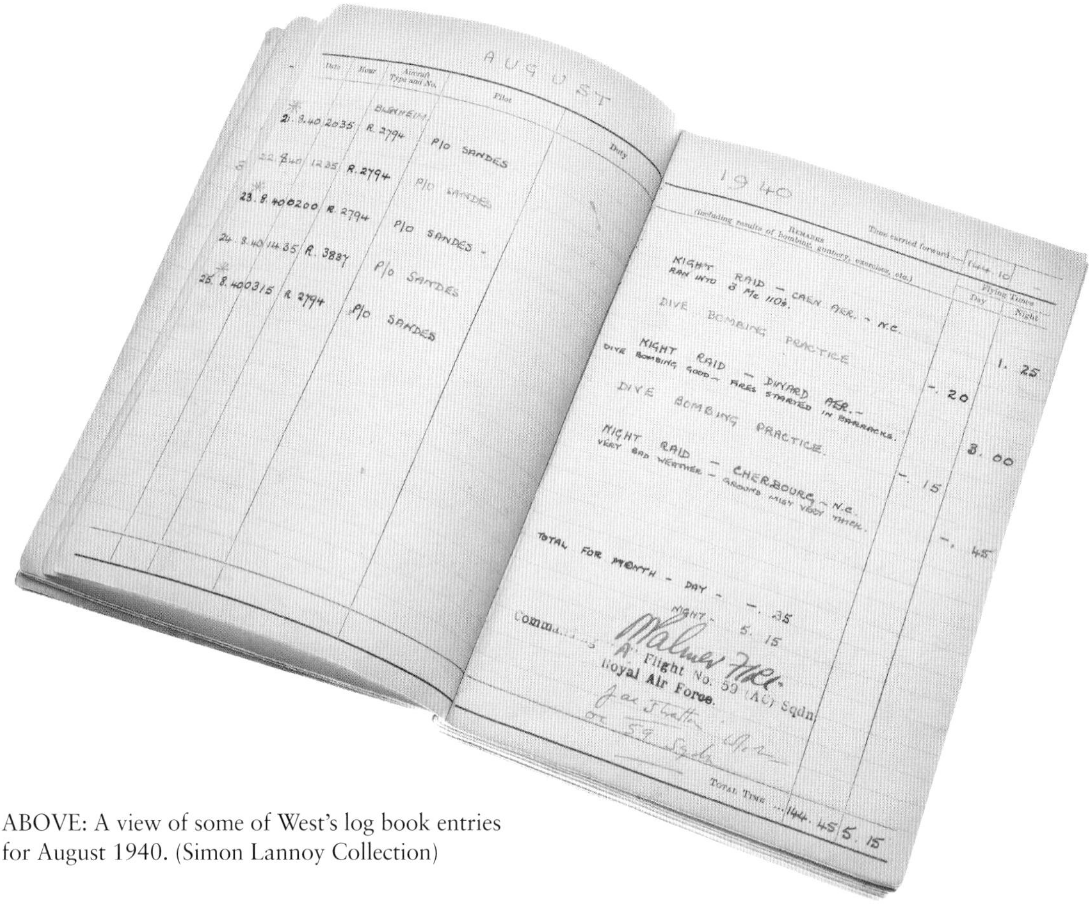

ABOVE: A view of some of West's log book entries for August 1940. (Simon Lannoy Collection)

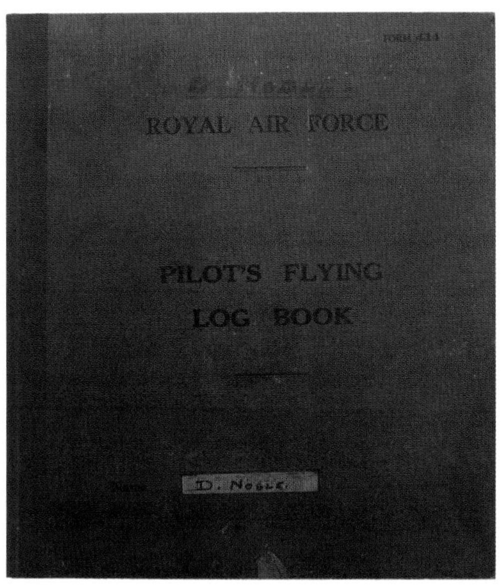

LEFT: The front of the Form 414 pilots' log book issued to Pilot Sergeant Dennis Noble. Noble, who originated from Retford in Nottinghamshire, had joined the Royal Air Force Voluntary Reserve, aged eighteen, in 1938. He learnt to fly at weekends and in his holidays and moved to London to work in a radio shop. He continued his flying training at Redhill aerodrome until he was called up at the beginning of the war in September 1939. Having completed his Hurricane training, Dennis was posted to his first squadron, No.43, the 'Fighting Cocks', which was at RAF Tangmere, on 3 August 1940. (Tangmere Aviation Museum)

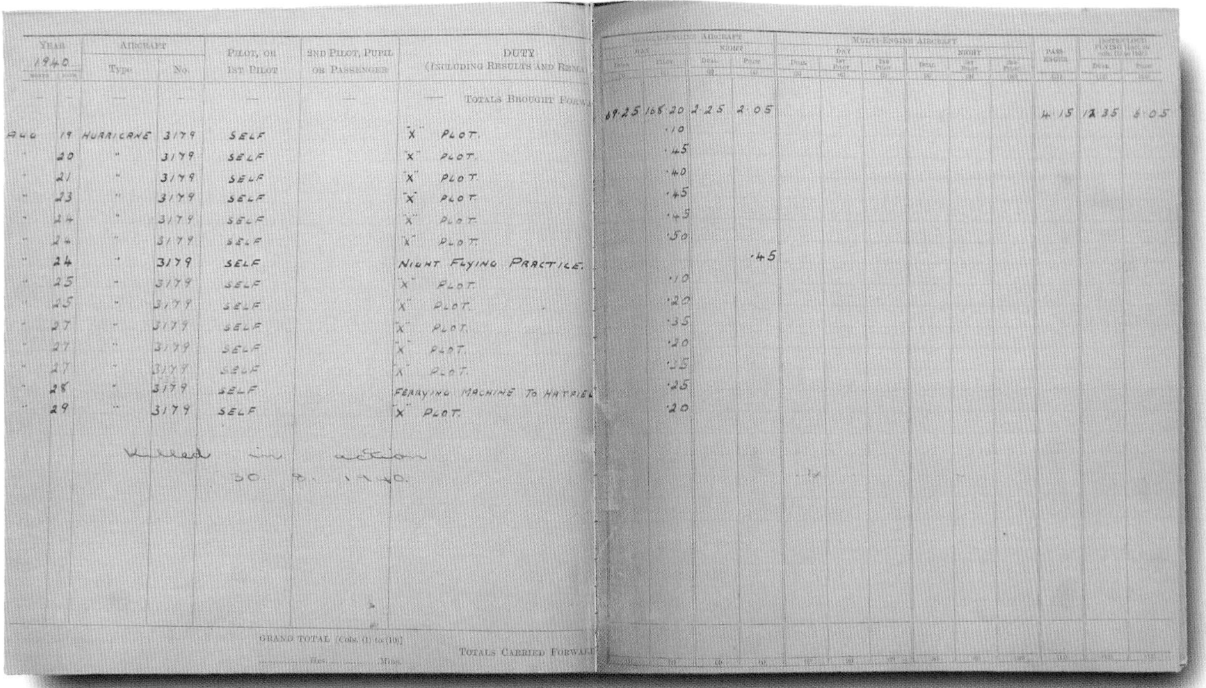

Year 1940 Month	Date	Aircraft Type	Aircraft No.	Pilot, or 1st Pilot	2nd Pilot, Pupil or Passenger	Duty (Including Results and Remarks)	Single-engine Day	Single-engine Night
						Totals Brought Forward	69.25 165.20	2.25 2.05
Aug	19	Hurricane	3179	Self		"X" Plot.	.10	
"	20	"	3179	Self		"X" Plot	.45	
"	21	"	3179	Self		"X" Plot	.40	
"	23	"	3179	Self		"X" Plot	.45	
"	24	"	3179	Self		"X" Plot	.45	
"	24	"	3179	Self		"X" Plot	.50	
"	24	"	3179	Self		Night Flying Practice.		.45
"	25	"	3179	Self		"X" Plot	.10	
"	25	"	3179	Self		"X" Plot.	.20	
"	27	"	3179	Self		"X" Plot.	.35	
"	27	"	3179	Self		"X" Plot.	.20	
"	27	"	3179	Self		"X" Plot.	.15	
"	28	"	3179	Self		Ferrying machine to Hatfield	.25	
"	29	"	3179	Self		"X" Plot.	.20	

Killed in action 30. 8. 1940.

The last entry in Pilot Sergeant Dennis Noble's log book is dated 30 August 1940. On that day, the squadron engaged enemy aircraft over East Sussex. At 11.50 hours Noble was seen to dive away from the battle, crashing into the pavement of Woodhouse Road, Hove. (Tangmere Aviation Museum)

OFFICIAL PUBLICATIONS

Officers and NCOs were required by *The King's Regulations* to be in possession of certain essential books for reference. In the case of the officers, this included the following:

- The King's Regulations and Air Council Instructions for the RAF (AP 958)
- Manual of Air Force Law (AP 804)
- RAF Pocket Book (AP 1081)
- RAF War Manual, Part 1 – Operations (AP1300)
- RAF War Manual, Part 2 – Organisation and training (AP 1301)
- RAF Flying Training Manual, Part 1- Landplanes (AP 129)

For Airmen pilots the list was slightly different, but included the following:

- Extract from The King's Regulations and Air Council Instructions – regulations relating to flying (AP 1334)
- RAF Flying Training Manual, Part 1 – Landplanes (AP 129)
- RAF Pocket Book (AP 1081)
- Aeroplane Maintenance Regulations (AP 1574)

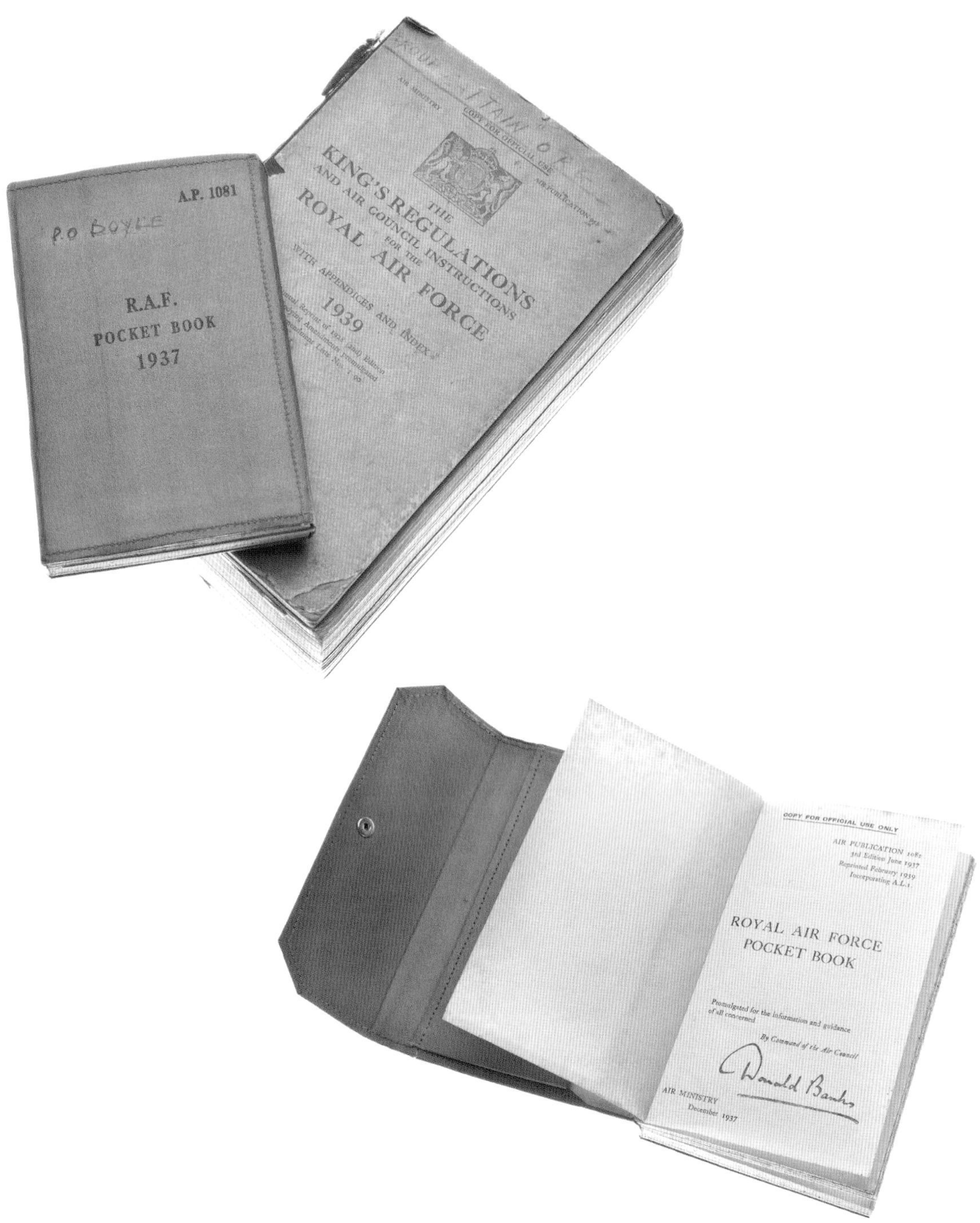

Amongst the 'essential' reading for aircrew are the two publication seen here – a set of the King's Regulations and Air Council Instructions for the RAF (AP 958) and the RAF Pocket Book (AP 1081), which contained a wealth of information including survival techniques, signals and the like. The pocket book is a February 1939 reprint of the 1937 edition which incorporated amendment AL1. It is this version that aircrew would have had during the Battle of Britain period. (Mark Hillier Collection)

MAPS

Despite the fact that maps or charts were in constant use by fighter pilots during the Battle of Britain, there was, surprisingly, little storage space for them in the cockpit. Often, they were of no use as after a very intense combat, a pilot could find himself miles away from their last known location with no idea of where they were.

Most issue maps comprised folded paper in a thick brown heavy paper cover. They were generally of the 4 miles to 1-inch, or ¼ inch to 1 mile, scale. There were twelve sheets that covered England and Wales, with a further ten for Scotland.

Maps are often seen in period photographs with the pilots carrying them in their flying boot as Wing Commander Geoffrey Page DSO, DFC, recalled: 'Returning to the hut I stuffed maps into the side of my black leather flying boots and a miniature compass into my breast pocket.'

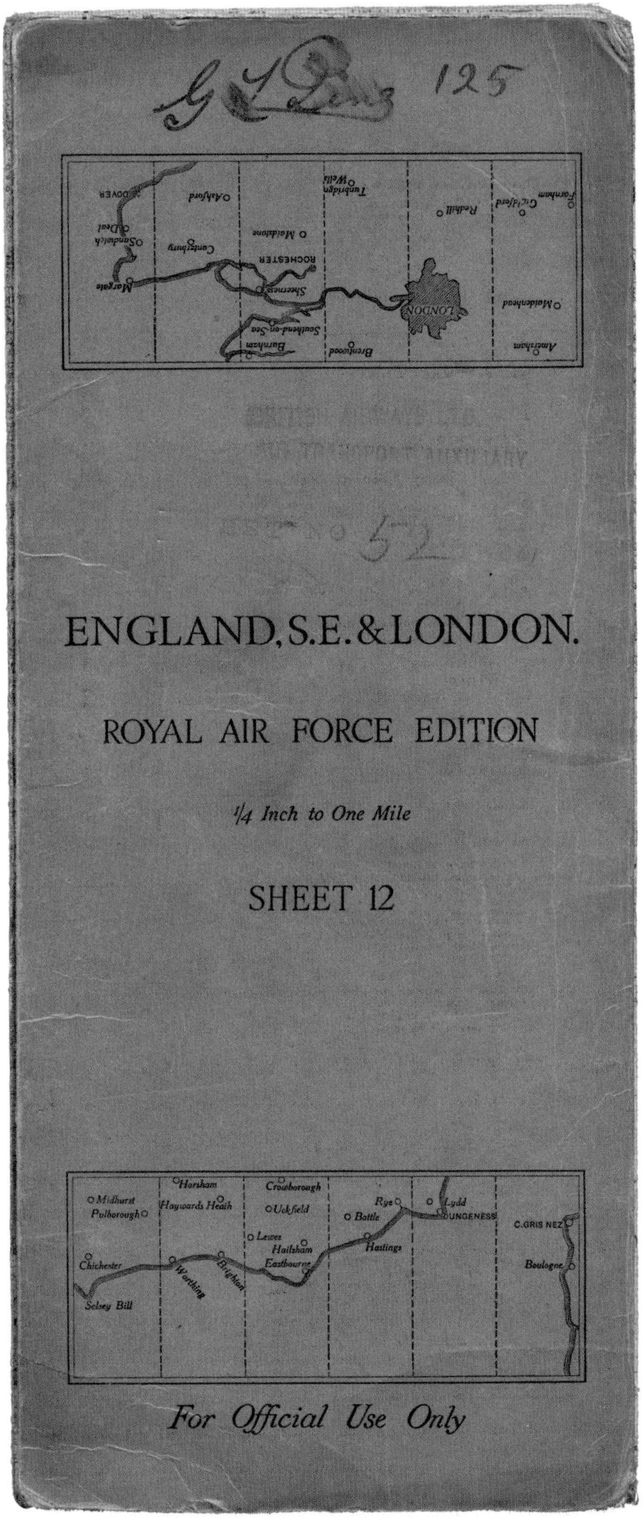

The front of an RAF issue map, in this case Sheet 12 which covered South East England and London at a scale of ¼-inch to one mile. The map has a card front and rear cover. The map folds down to a convenient size to tuck into a flying boot. (Mark Hillier Collection)

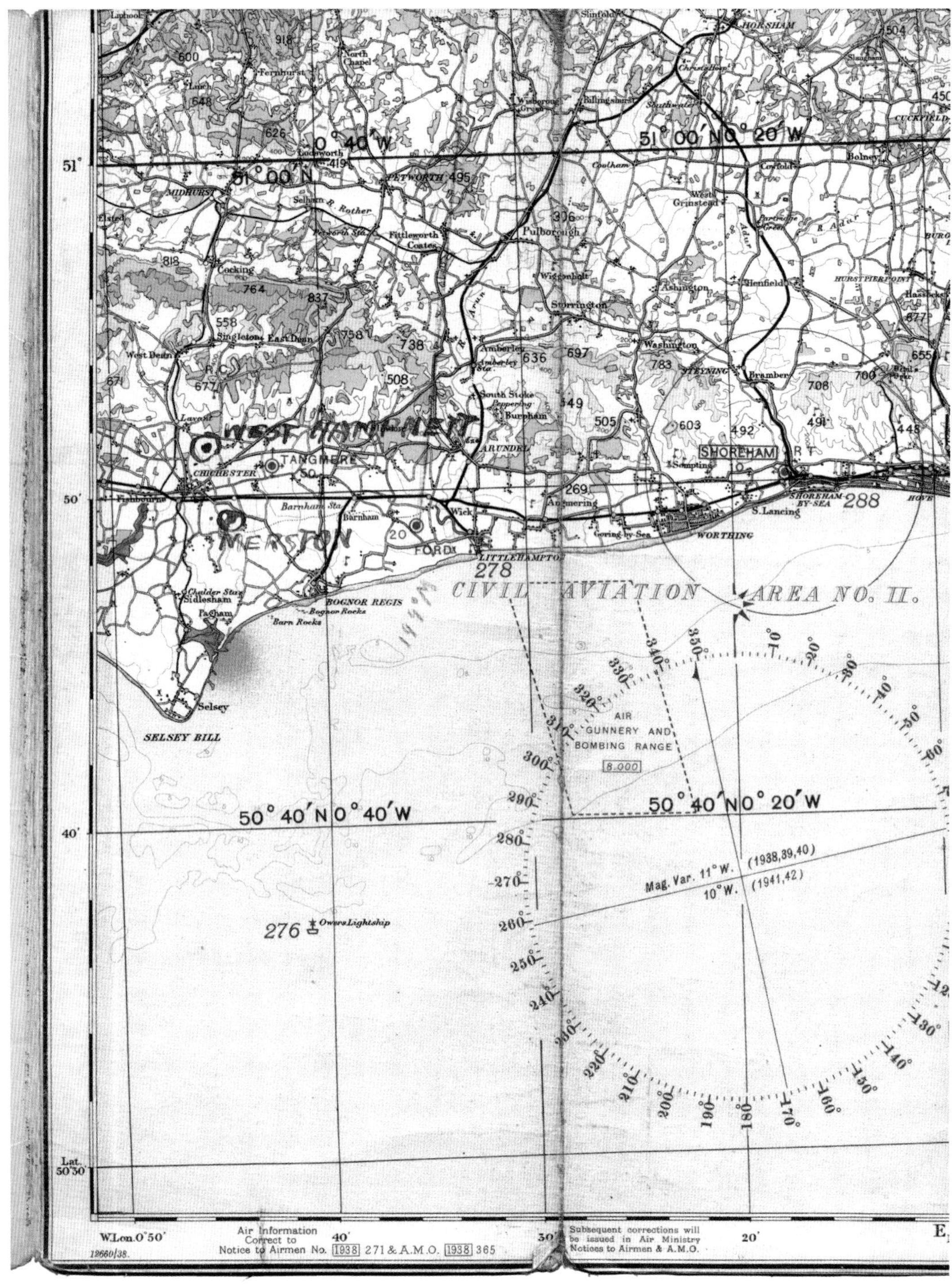

Detail on the Sheet 12 map. Military airfields are denoted by a red dot with a circle around it. However, both RAF Westhampnett and RAF Merston have been added by hand, indicating that whilst the map is dated 1938, it was still in use in 1940. (Mark Hillier Collection)

SERVICE REVOLVER

The standard issue sidearms available to officers during the Battle of Britain were the Webley .38 revolver or the Colt automatic pistol. However, most officers chose not to carry them and, at the discretion of the unit CO, they could deposit them in the station armoury.

>>>

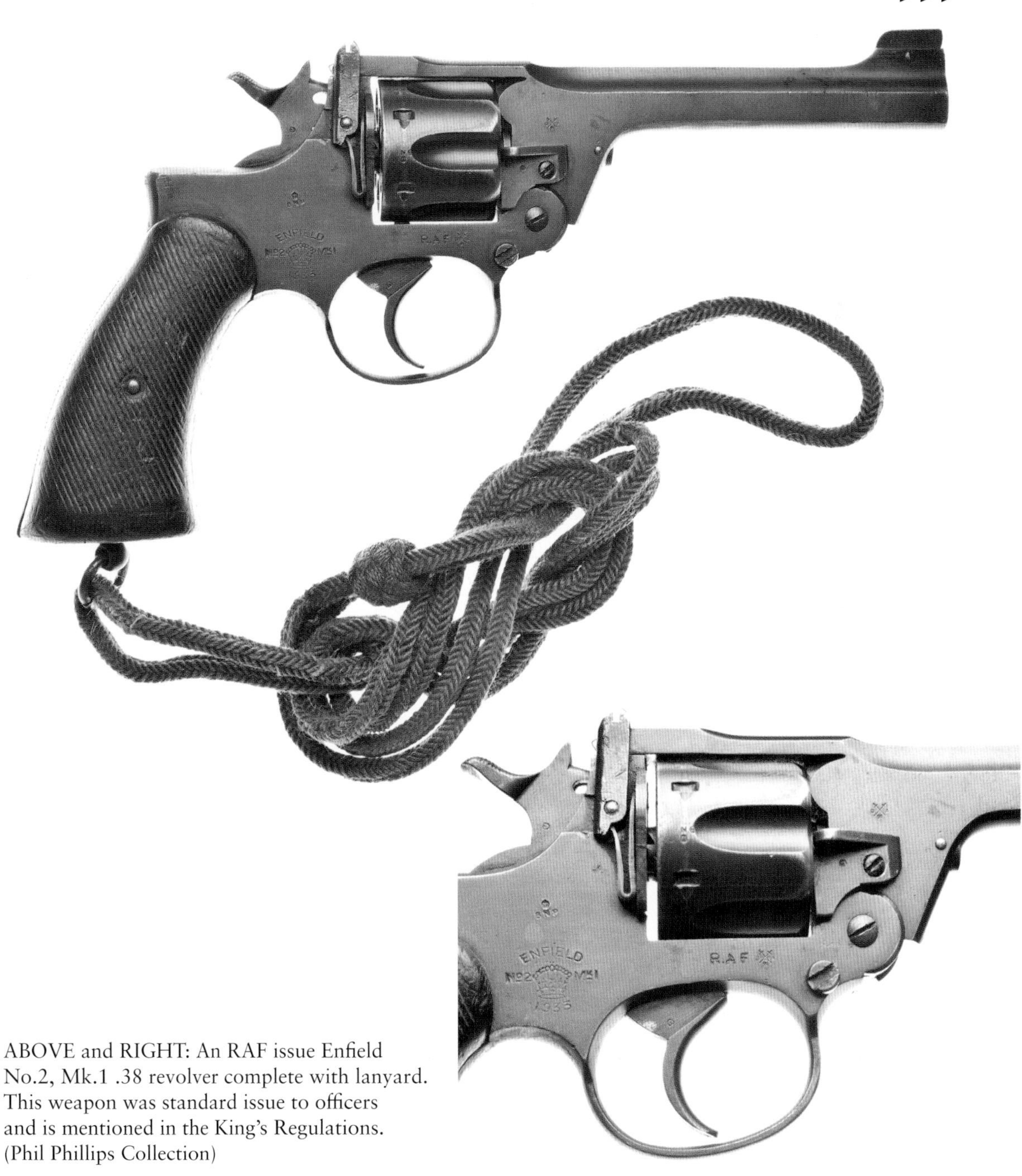

ABOVE and RIGHT: An RAF issue Enfield No.2, Mk.1 .38 revolver complete with lanyard. This weapon was standard issue to officers and is mentioned in the King's Regulations. (Phil Phillips Collection)

Paragraph 2566 of *The King's Regulations* states: 'Every officer of the general duties branch must be in possession of a service type of pistol or revolver throughout his period of service on the active list.' It adds that, 'every such officer, subject to clause 2, will be entitled to be issued on demand to No.1 Maintenance Unit, with one Colt automatic pistol (.455") or pistol revolver No.2, Mark 1 (.38") for his personal use during that period'.

These weapons would be carried in a 37 Pattern webbing holster on a webbing belt.

Some pilots flew with their sidearm, as Group Captain Thomas Gleave CBE once recalled. On the occasion in question, Gleave had been hit and his aircraft was on fire: 'The skin was already rising off my right wrist and hand, and my left hand starting to blister, the glove being already partially burned off. My shoes and slacks must have been burning at this time, but I cannot remember any great pain.

'I undid my harness and tried to raise myself, but found I had not the strength. I was comforted by the thought that I had my gun ready loaded if things came to the worst.'[27]

A 37 Pattern webbing belt and holster. (Phil Phillips Collection)

A portrait of a Great War veteran in his RAF Flying Officer's Volunteer Reserve uniform in the summer of 1940. Note the 37 Pattern webbing belt and revolver. (Mark Hillier Collection)

Section 9

BADGES OF RANK, CAP BADGES, FLYING BREVETS AND IDENTITY INSIGNIA

This section examines some of the different types of insignia and rank badges found on the uniforms of aircrew during the Battle of Britain. With personnel from different nationalities and air arms serving at this time, there was a variety of uniform insignia and flying badges in circulation.

In the RAF, for example, there were officers and NCO pilots who had been pre-war regulars. Then there were the Auxiliary Air Force pilots who, belonging to their own squadrons such as 602 (City of Glasgow) Squadron, were identified by the wearing of a brass 'A' on the uniform collar lapel. The Volunteer Reserve had started to form from 1936 onwards and had its own distinguishing insignia in the form of a brass 'VR', which was again worn by officers on the collar; NCO pilots a cloth version that was worn on the arm under the eagle on the shoulder.

The RAF's rank badges for officers were worn on the lower sleeves of the jacket and are a mixture of thin and thick rank braids to denote various ranks. For NCO aircrew, the lowest rank was sergeant, with the three stripes shown on the sleeves above the elbow. Flight sergeant rank was shown with a King's Crown above the centre of the 'V' of the sergeants' stripes. Warrant Officer pilots would have the Royal Arms and crown badge worn on the sleeves at the same position as the officers' rank.

All other nationalities flying for the RAF wore similar uniform and adopted the RAF ranks structure. The exception to this is that some Free French Air Force officers continued to wear their own uniforms.

For the Fleet air arm their rank was displayed on the end of the sleeves, formed of gold braid and sewn around the cuff.

NCO pilots wore a flying eagle in light blue embroidered thread, the background being either a dark blue or black oblong patch, on the left and right shoulder.

ABOVE: For those who joined the RAF Volunteer Reserve, the officers were required to wear small brass 'VR' badges on the collar. These are two different versions; one has tines that pierced the cloth and were then turned back, the other with lugs and a split pin. (Phil Phillips Collection)

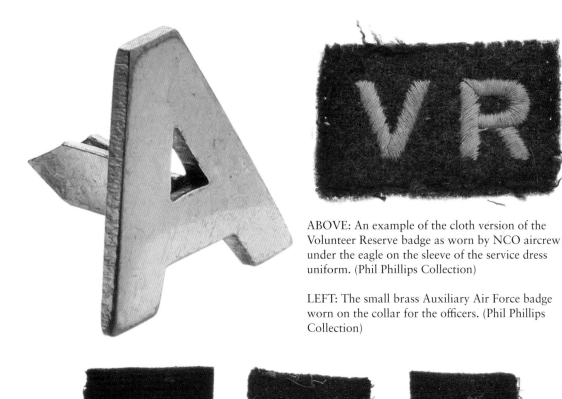

ABOVE: An example of the cloth version of the Volunteer Reserve badge as worn by NCO aircrew under the eagle on the sleeve of the service dress uniform. (Phil Phillips Collection)

LEFT: The small brass Auxiliary Air Force badge worn on the collar for the officers. (Phil Phillips Collection)

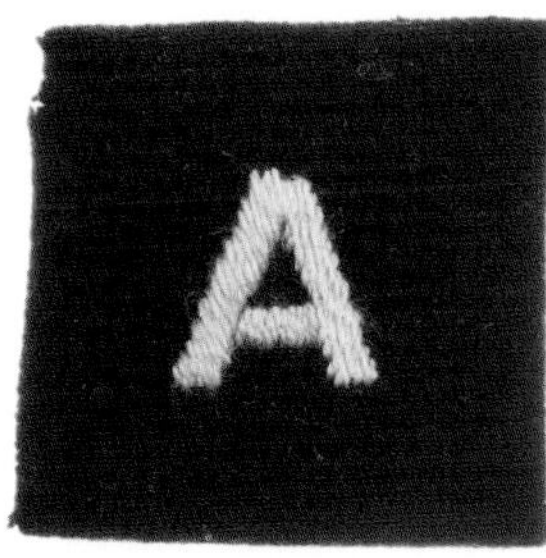

ABOVE: Three examples of the cloth Auxiliary Air Force badge which was worn under the eagle on the sleeve by NCO pilots and aircrew. (Phil Phillips Collection)

CAP BADGES

The cap badge used by an RAF NCO pilot on the field service cap was the standard brass RAF badge. The officer's field service cap had a brass RAF eagle with a King's Crown above; these were secured through the hat on to a plate behind the fabric or spacer, which kept the items in place with either three studs or lugs on the back.

The RAF officers' service dress hat badge was a gilt embroidered crown with red cushion, brass eagle and gilt laurel wreath on dark blue Melton wool which was a padded badge.

The RAAF cap badges were similar, apart from the NCO badge which had the monogram RAAF.

Warrant officer badges differed in that they were a gilt metal King's Crown, with a red cloth cushion within, under which was a flying eagle supported on four laurel sprigs. This would be worn on the service dress uniform hat, though the field service cap had the same badge as the officers'.

Fleet Air Arm pilots wore the standard Royal Navy officers' cap badge of a gold gilt embroidered Crown with surrounding laurels and anchor.

LEFT: The RAF officers' service dress hat badge was a gilt embroidered crown with a red cushion, brass eagle and gilt laurel wreath on dark blue woollen melton. (Simon Lannoy Collection)

RIGHT: A brass warrant officers' badge. Warrant officers would have worn a service dress hat similar to the officers' style, but with a patent black peak rather than the cloth covered version of the officers' type. The sergeant and flight sergeant aircrew at the time only wore the forage cap. (Phil Philips Collection)

ABOVE LEFT: The brass cap badge for NCO aircrew of the Royal Australian Air Force. (Phil Phillips Collection)

ABOVE RIGHT: The officers' gold braid cap badge for the Polish Air Force. (Phil Phillips Collection)

FLYING BADGES

For the trainee pilot of any air force, the focus of their attention would be to pass out from flying training and be able to sew on or wear the coveted flying badge which signified them as a qualified pilot. For the RAF trainees this meant they had to fulfil a number of criteria as laid down in *The King's Regulations*. This states:

> Officers, cadets and airmen undergoing the course of training at a flying training school or the RAF College must qualify as service pilots on the conclusion of their training. To qualify they must obtain not less than 50 per cent in the practical ground and air examinations in airmanship and maintenance, navigation, armament and reconnaissance, appropriate to the type of aircraft on which trained as laid down in the syllabuses for the flying training schools and the RAF College, and pass the following air tests:
> (a) Be able to fly consistently good compass course in clear air or in cloud;
> (b) Be able to fly at a steady height, course and speed accurately for periods of 5 minutes as for bombing;
> (c) Be able to climb with war load at or near maximum rate up to 15,000 feet or service ceiling if less
> (d) Be able to fly accurately in and position of a flight of three aircraft during take-offs and landings, climbs, dives and turns as appropriate to the type of aircraft;
> (e) Be able to take off and land consistently well by night.

As well as the above criteria, the pilot would have completed a minimum of eighty hours dual and solo flying, as well as be able to fly on instruments and demonstrate and execute aerobatic manoeuvres for the type being flown. Cross country flights also had to be conducted successfully with a triangular route of not less than 200 miles.

The RAF flying badge design dated back to the First World War and the Royal Flying Corps, although with a different monogram. The wings of the period consisted of the Tudor Crown, commonly known as the King's Crown, as it was used on RFC and RAF flying badges duriong both world wars. Under this is the nomogram 'RAF' surrounded by a wreath and wings sprouting from the sides, often with ten feathers on each side although there are variations.

The Battle of Britain period wings were mostly embroidered and padded wings on a black wool background, often found with a reinforcing mesh on the rear. It was always thought that the flat wings were mainly used by aircrew on the battledress which came into regular use in 1941, but examples of flat wings existed in the 1930s.

There were at least thirty-seven Australian pilots who were among 'The Few' who flew in the Battle of Britain in 1940. Most had trained in the pre-war RAAF and were on short service commissions with the RAF. They continued to wear the dark blue uniform of the RAAF with RAF insignia. Some wore the RAAF pilot's badge which had a blue wreath around the monogram RAAF.

In a similar vein, some of the New Zealand pilots who had been trained at home before coming to the UK retained NZ wings, though the majority appear to have relinquished their commissions in the RNZAF and joined the RAF, therefore qualifying for, and wearing, RAF wings. The situation was far from clear cut and variations occurred.

There were at least 145 Polish pilots who took part in the Battle, and whilst these pilots and aircrew were issued with RAF pilot's badges they also had their own wings. The latter took the form of a silver eagle in flight carrying a laurel wreath in its beak. Despite having a screw fastener on the rear, these badges were normally hung from a chain – but were often worn on the uniform without the chain, this being said to signify that 'the eagle was unchained and ready to fight'. These silver Polish wings are usually marked on the back with the manufacturer's name 'Knedler, Warsaw' on the back, although replacements and British variations can be found by companies such as J.R. Gaunt Ltd of London.

Of the other nations taking part in the Battle of Britain, Czechoslovakia contributed eighty-eight pilots. Their flying badge comprised a winged sword piercing a wreath of linden leaves and were die struck in silver with three fasteners which attached to loops on the uniform. The Czechoslovakian seal of a crowned rampant lion surmounts a diamond. The pilot badge was indicated by a gold wing and silver wreath.

Other nationalities wore RAF uniform and wings, but their nationality was signified by the use of a shoulder flash denoting the wearers' country of origin. During the Battle of Britain this mainly applied to Czech and Polish personnel as the other nationalities' shoulder flashes were not officially approved by the Air Ministry for wear until 1941. That said, it does appear that some Battle of Britain-dated photographs of No.1 RCAF Squadron exist showing officers with 'Canada' shoulder titles on their uniforms.

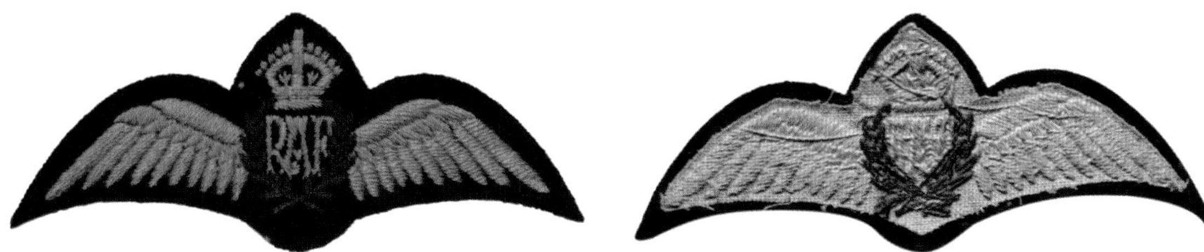

ABOVE LEFT and RIGHT: RAF pilots' wings showing the RAF monogram surrounded by a bronze embroidered wreath and King's Crown above. These are an example of the flat wings and, as can be seen from the reverse, tended to have a mesh for reinforcement. (Simon Lannoy Collection)

ABOVE: An example of the padded variety of King's Crown RAF wings. (Phil Phillips Collection)

BELOW: The RAAF pilots' wings differed from the RAF wings in the Monogram and also the surrounding wreath, which was pale blue in colour. (Phil Phillips Collection)

RIGHT: Flying Officer Paterson Clarence Hughes of 234 Squadron wearing his dark blue RAAF service uniform, complete with his RAAF wings. Note the eagle emblem above his rank braid on his arm.

ABOVE: Flight Lieutenant (later Group Captain) Desmond Sheen was an Australian who flew with the RAF during the Battle of Britain – he is seen here on the extreme left of this line-up of 72 Squadron pilots and aircraft at Acklington, Northumberland, in July 1941. The dark blue service dress uniform of the RAAF can clearly be seen in this image. Sheen was shot down twice during the Battle of Britain, in the course of which he accounted for three enemy aircraft destroyed, one shared, two probably destroyed and two damaged. (Kristen Alexander Collection)

BELOW LEFT and RIGHT: An example of the silver, Polish-produced aviators' badge. The badge is called 'gapa' and represents a silver eagle in flight with a laurel wreath in the beak. This is a screw-back example with a chain. Many were later produced by J.R Gaunt of London. (Phil Phillips Collection)

RIGHT: The Czechoslovakian aviators' badge consists of a winged sword piercing a wreath of linden leaves. The Czechoslovakian seal of a crowned rampant lion surmounts a diamond. The pilot badge was indicated by a gold wing and silver wreath. Pre-war examples were manufactured by Provaznik A. Spol in Prague – this being marked on the reverse. Later examples can be found to have been manufactured by Spink and Son of London. (Phil Phillips Collection)

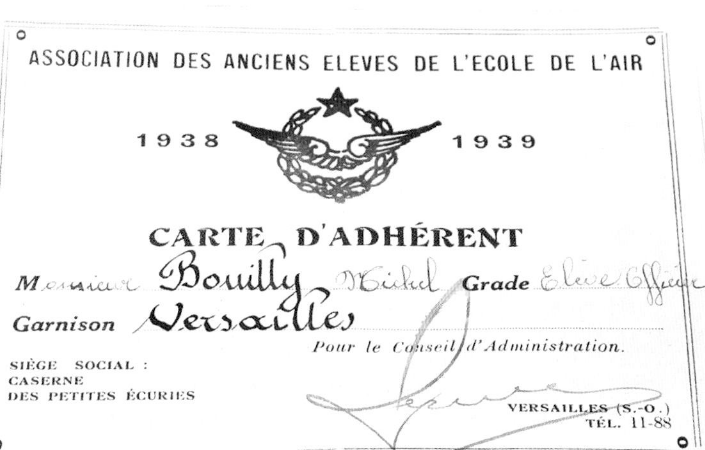

ASSOCIATION DES ANCIENS ELEVES DE L'ECOLE DE L'AIR

1938 1939

CARTE D'ADHÉRENT

Monsieur Bouilly Michel Grade Elève Officier

Garnison Versailles

Pour le Conseil d'Administration.

SIÈGE SOCIAL :
CASERNE
DES PETITES ÉCURIES

VERSAILLES (S.-O.)
TÉL. 11-88

ABOVE and RIGHT: A pre-war Armée de l'Air qualification badge and certificate to Michel Bouilly. (Phil Phillips Collection)

ABOVE: The King's Crown, Fleet Air Arm bullion wings as worn on the sleeve of the service dress uniform above the gold rank braid. (Phil Phillips Collection)

ABOVE and BELOW: Czechoslovakian shoulder titles of the type which were approved for wear on the service uniform. Those with the darker wool backgrounds tended to be for airmen, whilst the lighter barethea wool would have been for officers. (Phil Phillips Collection)

ABOVE and RIGHT: Polish shoulder titles as worn by aircrew, on the top of the arm, during the Battle of Britain.

OTHER FLYING BREVETS

The air gunners and observers who flew for Fighter Command in Bristol Blenheims and Bolton Paul Defiants had their own brevets consisting of a half-wing. Many of the air gunners had originated pre-war from the ranks and had come from trade backgrounds; they received additional pay for volunteering to be gunners. Such men wore a winged brass bullet badge on their sleeves to denote their role.

This situation was altered by Air Ministry Order A.416/40, which was dated 27 June 1940. From then on, all aircrew had to be at least of sergeant rank.

The air gunner brevet came into being in 1939, being authorised by Air Ministry Order A.547 1939. It was a half-wing with the monogram 'AG' surrounded by bronze embroidered laurel branch with the feathers extending up and to the right, all on a black backing.

At that stage in the war the role of navigator had not been established and most larger aircraft carried observers who were still wearing the winged 'O' brevet which had not changed in style since 1918. The pilot was responsible for the safe navigation of the aircraft but the observer assisted in navigation and also acted as the bomb aimer. Sometimes, a second pilot (usually a new pilot) acted as the observer to gain experience. The night fighter squadrons tended to operate with only two crew.

The other Blenheim Mk.IVF-equipped squadrons of Coastal Command, whose crews were eligible for the Battle of Britain Clasp, operated with a crew of three.

RIGHT: A cloth air gunner's half brevet which replaced the metal winged bullet originally worn by airmen who were paid extra to fly as gunners before the war. It was eventually decreed that all aircrew would hold the rank of sergeant and that the trade was formally recognised. This would have been worn by gunners in the rear of the Boulton Paul Defiant and in the Bristol Blenheim. (Simon Lannoy Collection)

ABOVE: A group of Blenheim air gunners, identifiable by their half brevets on their service dress uniform. The individual on the far left is wearing 1939 Pattern flying boots, which consisted of a canvas upper with leather strap. (Mark Hillier Collection)

LEFT: The observer half-wing which was worn in the early part of the war as the trade of navigator was not an individual one at the time. (Phil Phillips Collection)

REFERENCES

1. Bickers, Richard Townshend, *The Battle of Britain: The Greatest Battle in the History of Air Warfare* (Salamander Books Ltd, London, 1990).
2. Hillary, Richard, *The Last Enemy* (Macmillan, 1942).
3. Ross, David, *Stapme: The Biography of Squadron Leader Basil Gerald Stapleton DFC, DFC* (Grub Street, 2002).
4. Mayhew, E.R., *The Reconstruction of Warriors* (Greenhill Books, 2004).
5. Bickers, Richard Townshend, ibid.
6. Correspondence between Mick Prodger and the author.
7. Wellum, Geoffrey, *First Light: The True Story of the Boy Who Became a Man in the War-torn Skies above Britain* (Viking, 2002).
8. Levine, Joshua, *Forgotten Voices of the Battle of Britain* (Ebury Press, 2006).
9. ibid.
10. Neil, Tom, Wing Commander DFC & Bar, AFC, AE, *Gun Button to Fire* (William Kimber, London).
11. Levine, Joshua, ibid.
12. Air Publication 958, *The King's Regulations and Air Council Instructions for the Royal Air Force* (Air Ministry, 1939)
13. Corbin, James, Flight Lieutenant DFC, *Last of the Ten Fighter Boys* (Sutton Publishing, 2007).
14. Doe, Bob, Wing Commander DSO, DFC & Bar, *Bob Doe: Fighter Pilot* (CCB, 2004).
15. Air Publication 958, ibid.
16. Bickers, Richard Townshend, ibid.
17. Doe, Bob, ibid.
18. Corbin, James, ibid.
19. Kingcome, Brian, *A Willingness to Die: Memories from Fighter Command* (History Press, 2006).
20. Imperial War Museum (IWM), Department of Sound, recording reference 21117.
21. Page, Geoffrey DSO, DFC, *Tale of a Guniea Pig: The Exploits of a World War II Fighter Pilot* (Wingham Press, 1981).
22. Barthropp, Patrick, Wing Commander, *Paddy* (Howard Baker Press, 1987).
23. Darlow, Steve, *Five of the Few: Survivors of the Battle of Britain and the Blitz Tell Their Story* (Grub Street, 2006).
24. Hillier, Mark, Percival, Greg, and Sinanan, Dieter, *Westhampnett at War* (Yelloman Publishing, 2010).
25. Quill, Jeffrey OBE, CBE, *Spitfire: A Test Pilot's Story* (John Murray, 1983).
26. Wellum, Geoffrey, ibid.
27. Mayhew, E.R., ibid.

BIBLIOGRAPHY

Barber, Mark, *RAF Fighter Command Pilot: The Western Front 1939-42* (Warrior, 2012).

Barthropp, Patrick, Wing Commander, *Paddy* (Howard Baker Press, 1987).

Bickers, Richard Townshend, *The Battle of Britain: The Greatest Battle in the History of Air Warfare* (Salamander Books Ltd, 1990).

Corbin, James, Flight Lieutenant DFC, *Last of the Ten Fighter Boys* (Sutton Publishing, 2007).

Cormack, Andrew, *The Royal Air Force 1939-45* (Men-at-Arms, 1990).

Darlow, Steve, *Five of the Few: Survivors of the Battle of Britain and the Blitz Tell Their Story* (Grub Street, 2006).

Doe, Bob, Wing Commander DSO, DFC & Bar, *Bob Doe: Fighter Pilot* (CCB, 2004).

Hillier, Mark, *A Fighter Command Station at War* (Frontline Books, 2016).

Hillier, Mark, Percival, Greg, and Sinanan, Dieter, *Westhampnett at War* (Yelloman Publishing, 2010).

Hobart, Malcolm, *Badges and Uniforms of the RAF* (Pen & Sword, 2013).

Howard, Bill, *What the RAF Airman Took to War* (Shire, 2015).

Kingcome, Brian, *A Willingness to Die: Memories from Fighter Command* (History Press, 2006).

Levine, Joshua, *Forgotten Voices of the Battle of Britain* (Ebury Press, 2006).

Neil, Tom, Wing Commander DFC & Bar, AFC, AE, *Gun Button to Fire* (William Kimber, London).

North, Jonathon, *An Illustrated Encyclopaedia of Uniforms of World War II* (Lorenz Books, 2015).

Page, Geoffrey DSO, DFC, T*ale of a Guniea Pig: The Exploits of a World War II Fighter Pilot* (Wingham Press, 1981).

Prodger, Mick, *The Luftwaffe Vs. RAF: Flying Equipment of the Air War, 1939-1945* (Schiffer, 2004).

___________, *Trending Collectibles: 2015* (Military Aviation Review).

___________, *Vintage Flying Helmets: Aviation Headgear Before the Jet Age* (Schiffer, 2004).

Quill, Jeffrey OBE, CBE, *Spitfire: A Test Pilot's Story* (John Murray, 1983).

Ross, David, *Stapme: The Biography of Squadron Leader Basil Gerald Stapleton DFC, DFC* (Grub Street, 2002).

Wellum, Geoffrey, *First Light: The True Story of the Boy Who Became a Man in the War-torn Skies above Britain* (Viking, 2002).